Roman Britain

Life at the Edge of Empire

RICHARD HOBBS AND RALPH JACKSON

THE BRITISH MUSEUM PRESS

For our parents

And with grateful thanks to
Belinda Wilkinson, Jonathan Williams,
Stephen Crummy, John Williams,
Kevin Lovelock and Saul Peckham

Frontispiece Gold votive plaque from a temple hoard found
near Ashwell, Hertfordshire, 2nd to 3rd century AD.
Opposite Gold *aureus* (reverse) struck at Rome in AD 46 or 47
to celebrate the emperor Claudius' triumph over the Britons.

© 2010 Richard Hobbs and Ralph Jackson

First published in 2010 by The British Museum Press
A division of The British Museum Company Ltd
38 Russell Square, London WC1B 3QQ

Richard Hobbs and Ralph Jackson have asserted their right
to be identified as the authors of this work.

A catalogue record of this book is available
from the British Library.

The papers used in this book are natural, renewable and recyclable
products and the manufacturing processes are expected to conform
to the environmental regulations of the country of origin.

ISBN 978 0 7141 5061 1

Designed by Zoë Mellors
Printed in China

CONTENTS

Roman Britain

I

INTRODUCTION

Britain was a province at the far edge of the Roman Empire for almost four centuries, from AD 43 to about AD 410, during which time it was ruled by a Roman administration. This book reveals the distinctive Romano-British culture that developed over those centuries. It draws on evidence from both archaeological investigations

and ancient written sources, and integrates it with current research

on the surviving artefacts – the material remains – in the incomparable collections of the British Museum.

N O BOOK ON ROMAN BRITAIN can ignore the written evidence. Indeed, until the late nineteenth century, it was the principal source of information for those attempting to understand this period of our history. But there is rather little of it and, as it was written mainly by Greek and Roman geographers and historians, it lacks a British voice. As an assortment of anecdotal snippets and biased, partial and incomplete accounts, written evidence is often fascinating, but it falls far short of providing a balanced picture. Its main use is in the realm of political and military history.

Archaeology, by contrast, continues to surprise us with new, often unexpected discoveries, and contributes especially to our understanding of economic and social issues and the physical environment in which people lived (fig. 2). Forts, towns, villas, farms, temples and roads are among the many types of site revealed by archaeologists. Yet archaeological evidence is also biased, partial and incomplete, in part caused by the choice of sites examined, but also by the accident and nature of survival. Interpretation of the evidence is always necessary and seldom straightforward and there are very few undisputed 'facts'. So, archaeology and history complement and support each other in the light they shed on Roman Britain, but still the jigsaw lacks most of its pieces and we have to be careful not to push together pieces of evidence that do not fit. Some of the more exciting pieces are the objects that come from people's houses and workshops or belonged in public buildings, forts and temples. Large, small, costly, cheap, structural, portable, decorative or purely functional, all have the possibility of yielding new information. They can also speak to us directly about the people who made and used them some 2000 years ago.

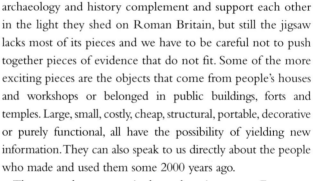

2 BELOW *The remains of buildings and objects painstakingly revealed by archaeologists bring us face to face with the debris of Romano-British life (© Amanda Clarke / University of Reading).*

Those people were no single unchanging group. For a start we are dealing with a large block of time, almost 400 years, a span similar to that between our own day and that of Shakespeare. During that time there were changes in such everyday things as dress and diet as well as in politics and the army. Britain's population also changed because it was part of a large empire and a wide range of incomers arrived over time, whether through military service, provincial administration or trade. Some brought families, some married locally and many settled in Britain. Some are known through inscriptions on tombstones or through particular burial customs, and others are occasionally detected through the distinctive objects they

left behind. But there was also continuity of
the way of life of the native Iron Age tribes
of Britain. Celtic names and designs (fig. 1)
persisted throughout the time that Britain
was a Roman province and are merely the
more durable or recognizable traces of the
'British' part of Romano-British culture.
Sometimes there was a fusion of Classical and
British traditions, as in the use of Classical
motifs adapted to British tastes or depicted in
'Celtic' style, whether in monumental stone
sculpture or in small bronze statuettes (fig. 3). The
impact of Roman culture varied enormously, from
monumental Classical-style buildings, in a few towns, or
religious shrines, to mosaic floors and frescoed walls in villas
(fig. 4), to the occasional imported pottery vessel found in the
more remote farms and villages. There was also a broad
geographical division, between the south-east, where most of
the towns and villas were concentrated, and the
north-west, where the great majority of the armed
forces were garrisoned, and these areas developed
their own different and distinctive ways of life (fig. 5).

*3 ABOVE In this British
take on Roman art, from
Kirkby Thore in Cumbria,
a lion overpowers a ram, a
common Roman symbol
of all-devouring death;
2nd to 3rd century AD.*

*4 BELOW Neptune
surrounded by dolphins,
crabs and mythical sea-
creatures — part of a suite of
floor mosaics from the villa at
Withington, Gloucestershire
(see also p. 7).*

Like other provinces of the empire, then, Britain was a
complex mixture of native people and incomers, soldiers and
civilians, who were united as subjects of Roman government

Inchtuthil

Carpow

Antonine Wall

Hadrian's
Wall

Carlisle

Vindolanda

Aldborough
YORK

Brough

Irish Sea

North Sea

Chester

LINCOLN

Caistor-by-
Norwich

Wroxeter
Leicester

Hoxne

Water
Newton

Mildenhall

Dolaucothi
Carmarthen

GLOUCESTER

COLCHESTER

Uley

Caerleon

Cirencester

St.
Albans

Caerwent

LONDON

Richboro

Bath

Lullingstone

Silchester

Canterbury

Winchester

Dover

Hod Hill

Bignor

Portchester

Chichester

Exeter

Dorchester

Fishbourne

English Channel

The Roman Empire about AD150

Mediterranean Sea

area under short-term or
sporadic military control

area probably under
long-term military control

area under civilian
administration

colonia

civitas centre

other town

other site

legionary fortress

fort

Saxon-shore fort

| 0 | 100 | 200 | 300 km |

| 0 | 100 | 200 miles |

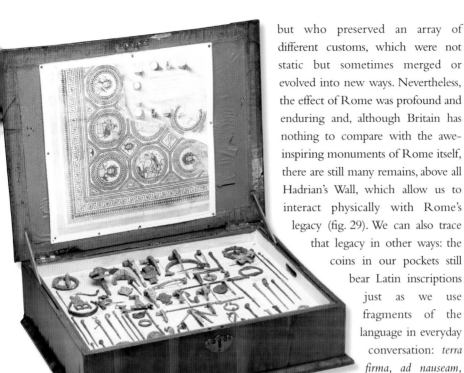

but who preserved an array of different customs, which were not static but sometimes merged or evolved into new ways. Nevertheless, the effect of Rome was profound and enduring and, although Britain has nothing to compare with the awe-inspiring monuments of Rome itself, there are still many remains, above all Hadrian's Wall, which allow us to interact physically with Rome's legacy (fig. 29). We can also trace that legacy in other ways: the coins in our pockets still bear Latin inscriptions just as we use fragments of the language in everyday conversation: *terra firma, ad nauseam, per diem, in vino veritas, et cetera* (!).

Many of today's buildings, too, show the influence of Rome – or at least Rome's adaptations of Greek architecture – including the British Museum, with its neo-classical façade and the colossal dome of its Round Reading Room inspired by Rome's Pantheon. Both are the result of the rediscovery of the Classical world, which inspired many British travellers on the Grand Tour during the Age of the Enlightenment. Some were prompted to write about the Classical past, some to record Roman Britain's remains. Others sought and collected surviving finds, whether portable and attractive objects, such as coins and jewellery (fig. 6), or more striking pieces such as stone altars and tombstones (fig. 59). With the establishment of the British Museum and an increasing interest in Britain's past, collections of Romano-British material began to be formed with vigour in the late nineteenth century. As the Roman Britain Gallery at the Museum and the many vivid illustrations in this book show, those collections, still expanding, help us to visualize in an ever more sophisticated way aspects of the rich and fascinating culture of Roman Britain.

5 OPPOSITE *Simplified map of Roman Britain (AD 43–c. 410) showing major roads, towns, forts, frontiers and other sites. Britain's position at the edge of the empire can be seen in the inset at top right.*

6 ABOVE *A box of curios and antiquities, mainly from Roman Britain, assembled during the Victorian period by William Allen (1808–97), a keen amateur collector.*

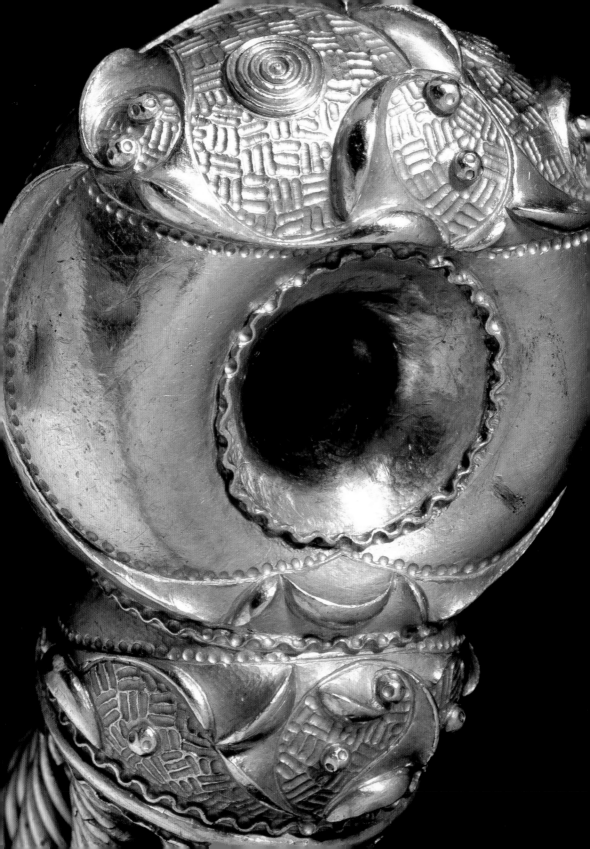

II

BRITONS
BEFORE ROME

'The inhabitants of Britain…. are especially friendly
to strangers and have adopted a civilized way of life
because of their interaction with traders and other
people. It is they who work the tin into pieces the
size of knucklebones and convey it to an island off
Britain, called Ictis… [where] merchants buy the tin
from the natives…'

Diodorus Siculus, *Library*, V, 22, c.30 BC

THE EARLIEST EVIDENCE for human habitation in Britain can be dated to around 700,000 years ago, when the British mainland was still connected to the continent by a land bridge. Long after the mainland had become separated from the continent by the English Channel about 8000 years ago, Britain was perceived by some as a land of mystery. Still as late as the time of the emperor Claudius (AD 41–54), there were people in Rome who refused to believe that *Britannia*, as the Romans knew it (a version of the earlier Latinized Greek *Pretannia*), even existed. Although the Channel proved at times to be an effective barrier to many would-be conquerors, it was never a decisive impediment to the ebb and flow of migration and trade, which has been a characteristic of British history for thousands of years.

Britain's political and cultural relationships with the continent and Ireland may have always been complex, but we can be certain that there have been few periods in the history of *Albion*, as it was first known (perhaps suggesting the white cliffs of Dover), when 'foreigners' were not

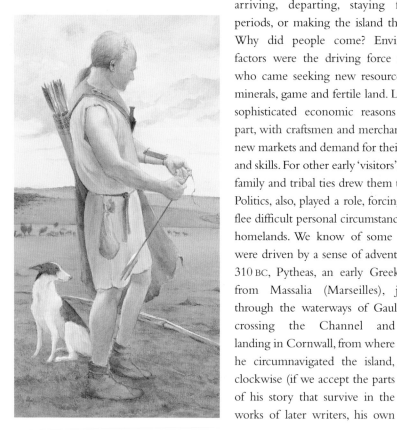

arriving, departing, staying for short periods, or making the island their home. Why did people come? Environmental factors were the driving force for many, who came seeking new resources such as minerals, game and fertile land. Later, more sophisticated economic reasons played a part, with craftsmen and merchants finding new markets and demand for their products and skills. For other early 'visitors', religious, family and tribal ties drew them to Britain. Politics, also, played a role, forcing some to flee difficult personal circumstances in their homelands. We know of some visits that were driven by a sense of adventure: about 310 BC, Pytheas, an early Greek explorer from Massalia (Marseilles), journeyed through the waterways of Gaul (France), crossing the Channel and landing in Cornwall, from where he circumnavigated the island, clockwise (if we accept the parts of his story that survive in the works of later writers, his own

7 LEFT *An artist's impression of the Amesbury Archer, an early metalworker buried near Stonehenge around 2,300 BC (© Wessex Archaeology/ Jane Brayne).*

account having been lost to us). But Britain as a source of mineral wealth was undoubtedly known from a very early date; tin, in particular, was a vital component for the manufacture of bronze, and led to the early establishment of trade links that brought islanders into contact with foreign customers. The Greek geographer Strabo, writing during the reign of the emperor Augustus (27 BC–AD 14), talks of the export of grain, cattle, gold, silver and iron, as well as 'hides and slaves, and dogs that are by nature suited to the chase' (*Geography*, IV, 5, 2, *c.* early first century AD).

Exchanges may have been made on islands off the south British coast, like Mount Batten in Devon, which has produced evidence for such prehistoric settlement and trade, and might indeed be the 'Ictis' referred to by Diodorus Siculus, a Greek historian writing in the first century BC (see p. 13).

As for the inhabitants of Britain during the Bronze Age (*c.*2,500–800 BC) and Iron Age (*c.*800 BC–AD 43), we can get a broad sense of what life was like. For the vast majority, it was a simple matter of subsistence farming, revolving around the growing of arable crops and the raising of livestock, with seasonal foodstuffs supplementing the diet. Gathering parties ventured beyond the boundaries of their communities to obtain resources like timber for fuel and building, salt for preserving food and suitable stone for making querns to grind corn. This would inevitably have brought them into contact with other groups, resulting in either peaceful exchanges of surpluses or violent conflicts. In time, such contacts led to regional diversity, whereby different social groups sought to distinguish themselves through different styles of dress and behaviour.

The British landscape by the middle of the third millennium BC was

8 ABOVE *Gold cup, c.1,600 BC, found at Ringlemere, Kent. Although crushed and distorted, the cup, probably for ceremonial use, is a remarkable survival of the Bronze Age.*

largely deforested, at least in the lowland areas, and people lived in open settlements, rarely heavily fortified, with an emphasis on timber dwellings with thatched roofs, although some buildings constructed of drystone walls are known in some regions, such as the south-west peninsula. The roundhouse was the commonest domestic structure in the Iron Age, although rectangular structures also existed, for instance, raised buildings, probably used to store grain. The majority of roundhouse entrances have been found to be orientated towards the sunrise, a means perhaps of tracking the progress of both day and the seasons, extremely important in times long before the invention of clocks and calendars. So, although life may have been simple, people had sophisticated ideas of the passage of time and the movement of the earth and the heavenly bodies.

Indeed for both the Bronze and Iron Ages, there is ample evidence of sophisticated beliefs and communal cooperation. Stonehenge, the most iconic of a huge number of monuments scattered across prehistoric Britain, was erected around 2,500 BC, and required a considerable amount of collective organization, not least in the transportation of the bluestones all the way from Pembrokeshire in west Wales. And we can also be fairly certain that it was the sacred landscape of Stonehenge that brought an early metal worker all the way from the Alps to his final resting place, providing archaeologists with one of the most extraordinarily rich finds of recent years (fig. 7). The 'Amesbury Archer', as he was nicknamed on account of the large number of flint arrowheads found in his grave, grew up in central Europe, perhaps Switzerland (as indicated by strontium levels in his teeth), yet he died and was buried, in about 2,300 BC, on Salisbury Plain, in sight of the standing stones.

The Amesbury Archer's grave contained gold ornaments and a copper knife. This is the earliest metalwork known from Britain; and, if he were able to extract metal from stone and shape it into tools and ornaments, it could have marked the Amesbury Archer out as something akin to a magician. The production of gold objects such as drinking vessels (fig. 8) alongside tools and weapons of copper and bronze, distinguishes the Bronze Age from earlier times when only stone (especially flint) was used. During the Iron Age (c.800 BC–AD 43), iron became more common for the manufacture of tools, weapons and other items such as chariot fittings, not necessarily because of a preference for its qualities over bronze, but because of its wider availability in comparison to tin and copper, the constituent elements of bronze. Nevertheless, in relative terms, we see an explosion in material culture, particularly during the late Iron Age (c.300 BC–AD 43), alongside changes in the nature of settlements.

One of the key features of this period is the emergence of the hillfort, mainly in the south of Britain, with the earliest constructed around 600 to 400 BC. Although of considerable variation in terms of size and shape, every hillfort is characterized by earth ramparts encircling a high point in the landscape: Maiden Castle in Dorset remains one of the most visually impressive (fig. 9). For many years, hillforts were thought to be primarily defensive structures in an increasingly tribal, warlike society, but recent studies have challenged this idea. Many archaeologists now believe that hillforts were not continuously occupied and would have been easily overrun by a concerted attack, so the 'defences' seem to have been largely symbolic. Instead, hillforts seem to reflect a communal version of the small-scale enclosures in which families and kin groups lived, and were used for the collective storage of grain, the distribution of foodstuffs and the exchange of surpluses such as sheep and cattle. Some sites, like Danebury in Hampshire, have also produced evidence of localized craft production such as metalworking. Hillforts may also have been used on 'special occasions', such as the summer solstice, and at these events people may have gathered to share food, participate in ceremonial activities, make religious offerings or honour their ancestors.

Some discoveries dated to the late Iron Age may relate directly to these ceremonial occasions. The most celebrated site is Snettisham near the north Norfolk coast, one of the few 'high points' in the East Anglian landscape. Inside what was probably a temple precinct, a series of torcs or neck-rings of gold, silver and base-metal, along with some coins and scrap metal, were buried in a series of carefully dug pits from perhaps the late second to

10 BELOW *The 'Great Torc' from Snettisham, Norfolk, one of the most elaborate golden objects known from the ancient world; early 1st century BC (see also p. 13).*

the first century BC. The 'Great Torc' from Snettisham (fig. 10) represents the pinnacle of Iron Age gold-working skill, craftsmanship and artistic originality: it also exudes power, status, and even magic, for torcs may have been regarded as possessing 'otherworldly' powers, as do other beautifully crafted items, such as mirrors (fig. 11). In this context it is interesting to note what Strabo writes about the Druids, whose responsibilities are believed to have included acting as priests in religious ceremonies and as judges in criminal cases: 'They [the Druids] not only wear gold ornaments – both chains round their necks and bracelets round their arms and wrists…' (*Geography*, IV, 4, 5).

11 ABOVE *Bronze mirror, from Desborough, Northamptonshire; one of the most finely decorated mirrors of the late Iron Age.*

We cannot associate Snettisham directly with the Druids, but it is clear that the burial of this extraordinary quantity of precious metal was carried out with care and purpose, perhaps as an offering to the gods and natural spirits, reflecting religious ideas that continued to develop into the Roman period (see chapter VIII). Although of later date (early to mid-first century AD), we see a similar burial of large quantities of precious metal, this time in the form of a series of coin hoards, at a site on high ground near Market Harborough in East Leicestershire, alongside large quantities of animal bone, the remains of communal feasts. The most curious items buried are parts of Roman cavalry helmets: their presence is difficult to explain, but shows the impact that the Roman world was having on Iron Age society (fig. 12).

Roman Britain is generally said to 'begin' in AD 43, when the emperor Claudius invaded and annexed the island as a new province (see chapter III). Yet in reality, the process of 'Romanization' had already started about a century earlier; and, as we have seen, contacts with the Mediterranean world go back further still. According to the Greek biographer Plutarch, the subjugation of the population of Gaul, during an eight-year campaign by the Roman general Julius Caesar (b. 100–d. 44 BC), was bloody and brutal. Caesar is said to have captured and looted more than 800 settlements, and slaughtered or enslaved a large proportion of the native Gallic population. In 55 BC, Caesar turned his attention to Britain. After one failed attempt to invade the island – much of his fleet was wrecked by storms – he returned again the following summer. The exact motivation for Caesar's campaigns in Britain is not clear: in his own writings, he simply states that the Gauls had 'received reinforcements from the Britons', so he probably sought to stem the flow of mercenaries (*The Gallic War*, IV, 20, *c.* mid-first century BC). A political motivation is very likely as well, for conquering Britain and 'taming' the Channel would have considerably bolstered Caesar's standing in Rome. But Caesar cannot have been unaware of the mineral riches of the island and the potential for other spoils of war, such as tribute and slaves. The size of Caesar's second expeditionary force tells us that he certainly meant business: his fleet was composed of 800 ships carrying over half his army (about 25,000 foot soldiers) and 2,000 cavalry. Only instability in Gaul led Caesar to abandon his second campaign. He advanced not much further than the Thames before turning back.

Caesar makes some interesting observations about the Britons he encountered: 'All the Britons, indeed, dye themselves with woad, which produces a blue colour, and make their appearance in battle

12 ABOVE *An iron, silver-clad cheek-piece from a Roman cavalry helmet, early 1st century AD, found near Market Harborough, Leicestershire. It depicts a Roman cavalryman being crowned by Victory and trampling a cowering barbarian.*

more terrible.' (*The Gallic War*, V, 14). Unfortunately, his account has led to the false impression that all ancient Britons were continuously covered in blue paint. Caesar also described in some detail, and no little admiration, the Britons' use of chariots, and their ability 'even on a declining and steep

13 ABOVE *A modern reconstruction of an Iron Age chariot, based on one found in a burial at Wetwang, East Yorkshire, from the 3rd century BC (© Tony Spence).*

place, to check their horses at full speed, and manage and turn them in an instant'. The importance of the horse-drawn chariot to Iron Age society is also attested archaeologically, with the discovery of chariot burials dated to the third century BC in East Yorkshire, for example at Wetwang (fig. 13).

The suggestion has been made that Caesar left troops in Britain, but this is not historically or archaeologically attested. What we know is that, in his memoirs, he tells us that 'deputies came to him from several states in the island with promises to give hostages and to accept the empire of Rome' (*The Gallic War*, IV, 33). Caesar certainly installed one 'puppet' government under the leadership of a Gallic chief Commios (see pp. 23, 26), who appears to have founded a dynasty in the south of Britain, in the tribal area of the Atrebates, approximating to modern Hampshire (fig. 14).

Whatever Caesar's legacy was in reality, we know that the next century saw a real change in the nature of the politics and culture of Britain. For

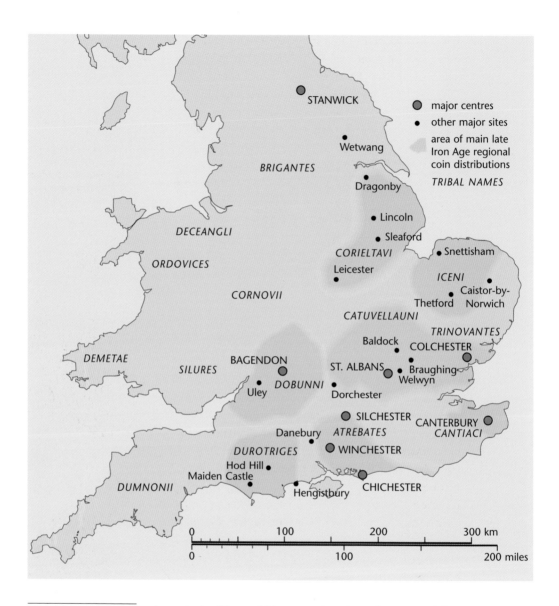

STANWICK

● major centres
• other major sites
░ area of main late
Iron Age regional
coin distributions
TRIBAL NAMES

• Wetwang

BRIGANTES

• Dragonby

• Lincoln

DECEANGLI

• Sleaford

CORIELTAVI • Snettisham

ORDOVICES

Leicester
•

ICENI •
Caistor-by-
Thetford Norwich
•

CORNOVII

CATUVELLAUNI

TRINOVANTES

Baldock
•

COLCHESTER ●

DEMETAE

BAGENDON

ST. ALBANS ● • Braughing
Welwyn
•

SILURES

●
DOBUNNI
Uley • • Dorchester

• SILCHESTER CANTERBURY ●

Danebury *ATREBATES* *CANTIACI*
•

DUROTRIGES ● WINCHESTER

Hod Hill •
Maiden Castle •

CHICHESTER ●

DUMNONII

Hengistbury
•

| 0 | 100 | 200 | 300 km |
| 0 | | 100 | 200 miles |

14 ABOVE *Simplified map of
southern Britain in the late
Iron Age, c. mid-1st century
BC to mid-1st century AD.*

the majority, life would have continued much as normal, but
for others we can find signs of the embracing of 'Roman
ways' and the forging of political alliances that undoubtedly
paved the way for the Claudian invasion (chapter III).
Evidence suggests that Britain by the late first century BC consisted of a
number of tribal states, each with a particular geographical zone of
influence. How these 'tribes' were structured is rather unclear and, in

any case, varied throughout the island. We know from coinage that some rulers, such as Cunobelin (immortalized as Shakespeare's *Cymbeline*), styled themselves *REX*, meaning 'king', which would suggest that ultimate power lay in the hands of one individual (fig. 15). Indeed, Cunobelin, who appears from the spread of his coinage to have ruled a kingdom covering much of the area north of the Thames, is referred to as *Rex Britannorum*, 'King of the Britons', by the historian Suetonius (*Lives of the Caesars*, IV, 44). But, in other parts of Britain, coins often display pairs of names, suggesting a different way of ruling. Women, too, seem to have wielded political and military power to a greater extent than we might expect: Cartimandua, in power perhaps even before Claudius' invasion in AD 43, was 'queen' of the Brigantes, the largest tribe in Britain occupying the greater part of northern England, whilst Boudica is probably the most famous ancient Briton of all (see chapter III).

15 BELOW *Silver coin struck by Verica, a British tribal leader of the early 1st century* AD. *The coin is inscribed* VERICA REX COMMI F, *Latin for 'King Verica, son of Commios'.*

One of the features of the late Iron Age is a substantial rise in Mediterranean imports. At Heybridge in Essex for example an Iron Age settlement on the east coast, excavations have produced the largest assemblage of wine amphorae of the first century BC north of the Thames, suggesting that Heybridge may have been one of the ports for the export of goods to the Continent. In a burial chamber at Welwyn Garden City, the cremated remains of perhaps a tribal chief were accompanied by no less than five amphorae, alongside a range of imported drinking vessels including an Italian silver wine cup (fig. 16). The wine itself is likely to have been drunk during the funeral rituals. At other sites, such as Stanway and Lexden in Essex, amphorae were smashed after drinking and pieces from the containers carefully selected for inclusion in the grave.

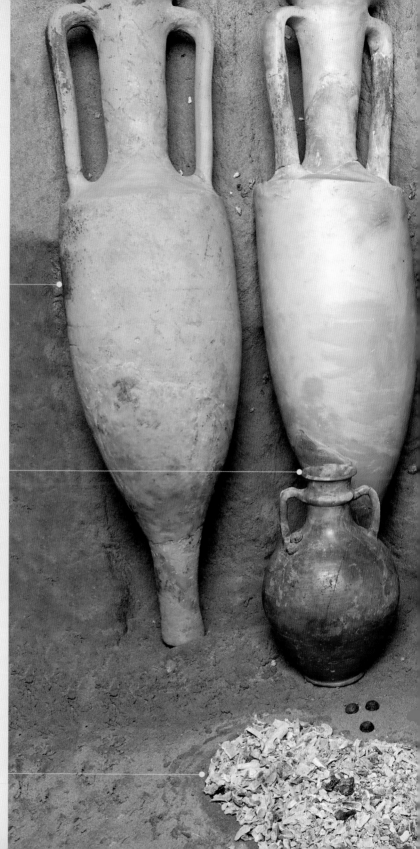

16 An Iron Age burial discovered at Welwyn Garden City, Hertfordshire in 1965.

AMPHORA (JAR),
*one of five found in
the grave, probably
used to transport
wine from Italy.*

CLAY FLAGON
*for pouring wine, or perhaps
beer, to sustain the grave's
occupant during the afterlife.*

GLASS GAMING PIECES,
*made in the eastern
Mediterranean, possibly
for a game similar to Ludo.*

BONES *of the grave's
occupant, an important man
or woman, who was wrapped
in a bear skin, and then
cremated.*

IN FOCUS

IRON AGE BURIAL

LATE 1ST CENTURY BC

WHITE-SLIP FLAGON, *made of clay with a white-slipped surface, probably imported from the Continent.*

DRINKING VESSELS *produced locally in clay.*

BRONZE DISH, *with a drop handle (to its left), and two ceramic vessels inside. The dish may have contained an offering of food for the deceased.*

SILVER DRINKING CUP, *imported from Italy, one of the finest objects in the grave. Similar cups have been found at Pompeii.*

In 2001, an important discovery was made near Winchester in Hampshire (fig. 17). Comprising a set of what might be described as 'his and hers' jewellery of mid-first century BC date, its quality and style hints at political ties between Rome and Britain. The hoard contains, in addition to a pair of gold brooches and plain gold cuff bracelets, two beautiful woven necklaces of refined gold wire. The necklaces are lithe and flexible, completely different to those found at Snettisham (see pp. 18–19). Most importantly, the quality and style of the gold work suggests production in a workshop sited perhaps in the eastern Mediterranean. How these extraordinary objects ended up being buried in Hampshire is not known, but it is possible they were a diplomatic gift, perhaps to an Atrebatic tribal leader and his 'queen'. Local rulers of the Atrebates, such as Tincomarus, Verica and Eppillus, claimed descent from Commios (see pp. 21, 23), employed Roman imagery and used Latin on their coinage (fig. 15). Both the coinage evidence and the Winchester discovery suggest strong links with the Roman ruling elite and, indeed, Verica is thought to have fled to Rome in about AD 42 after an unrecorded episode of local strife (Cassius Dio, *Roman History*, LX, 19, *c.* AD 220).

Southern Britain by the early first century AD was therefore very much aware of the proximity of Rome. Some tribal leaders seem to have embraced Roman culture as a result and actively sought to align themselves politically. But Rome clearly felt that Britain remained a threat, and had enough natural wealth for it not to be ignored. For these reasons, Augustus, the first Roman emperor, considered an invasion on at least three occasions. Then in AD 40, Gaius (Caligula) (AD 12–41), too, readied an army, but in typical style for his reign, the campaign was aborted. Nevertheless an invasion was imminent, and Britain would soon cease to be a mysterious, mist-shrouded island on the edge of the known world.

17 RIGHT *Set of gold jewellery, found near Winchester, Hampshire, probably made in the east Mediterranean, during the late 1st century BC.*

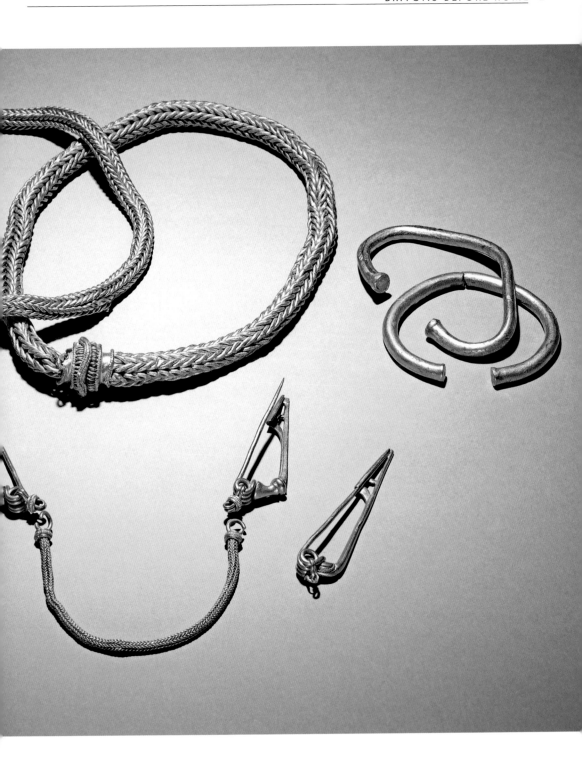

III

INVASION AND CONQUEST

'So it was that Plautius undertook the expedition, though he had difficulty in getting his army to leave Gaul, since the troops were indignant at the prospect of campaigning outside the known world...'

Cassius Dio, *Roman History,* LX, 19, about AD 220

IN THE SUMMER OF AD 43 Aulus Plautius, commander-in-chief for the emperor Claudius, assembled an army of invasion at Boulogne (fig. 18). It was, for its day, a huge force, and one that included many experienced senior military officers, an indication of the scale and difficulty of the task anticipated. Four legions and numerous auxiliary units – around thirty to forty thousand men in total – prepared to embark.

The invasion of Britain was designed to crush resistance, exploit the mineral and human resources of the country and bring Claudius a great military triumph. Just at that moment the army faltered, indignant and apprehensive, we are told, at the prospect of their campaigning 'outside the limits of the known world'. It took the sarcasm of one of Claudius's freed men to shame the troops into action, an inauspicious start to an invasion, which lasted far longer than anyone could have believed possible.

18 ABOVE *The emperor Claudius (AD 41–54), in his glory, on a gold* aureus *struck at Rome in AD 46 or 47 to celebrate his invasion of Britain.*

In the event, the soldiers' fears proved unfounded and the Channel crossing was accomplished without mishap. The only surviving written source for the invasion is that of the Greek historian Cassius Dio. It seems that the army sailed in three squadrons, probably to Kent, though some have postulated a landfall in the Solent. Their landing was uncontested, but they soon met with concerted British resistance, led by Caratacus and Togodumnus, two sons of the tribal leader Cunobelin (see p. 23). There are accounts of serious battles at two river crossings, the second undoubtedly the Thames, the first thought by some to be the Medway. On both occasions Roman specialist units – auxiliaries who could swim in full kit – helped to tip the balance and ensure Roman victory. After the British defeat, Caratacus fled westwards to continue the struggle. Meanwhile, Aulus Plautius sent news to Rome, and Claudius came to Britain – with an entourage that included elephants – to lead his victorious army in the capture of the Catuvellaunian stronghold at Colchester and accept the submission of eleven British 'kings'. After just sixteen days in Britain, Claudius left Plautius to complete the conquest and returned to Rome to celebrate his triumph in AD 44, in the words inscribed on his triumphal arch in Rome, as 'the first to bring barbarian nations beyond the Ocean under Roman sway' (fig. 19).

But it was not to be as easy as that. With base and flanks relatively secure through conquest and through alliances – especially with the Iceni in Norfolk and the Regni in Sussex – Plautius appears to have taken forward the invasion on several fronts. Leaving Legion XX in the Colchester region to stabilize the newly-won territory and construct a fortress, he divided his army into battle-groups, which advanced simultaneously into the south-west, west, and north-east.

Led, respectively, by complete or substantial parts of Legions II Augusta, XIV Gemina and IX Hispana, these battle-groups combined legionary and auxiliary soldiers, in order to capitalize on particular qualities and specialist fighting skills geared to terrain and enemy numbers. Legion II Augusta, which spear-headed the campaign in the south-west, was commanded by the future emperor Vespasian. One of the British hill-forts taken by his troops was Hod Hill, in Dorset, where excavations from 1951–8 revealed the Roman fort that was subsequently

19 BELOW *Reverse of the gold coin in fig. 18 (opposite), showing Claudius' monumental arch in Rome, complete with a statue of the emperor on horseback, and with the abbreviation DE BRITANN, referring to his triumph over the Britons.*

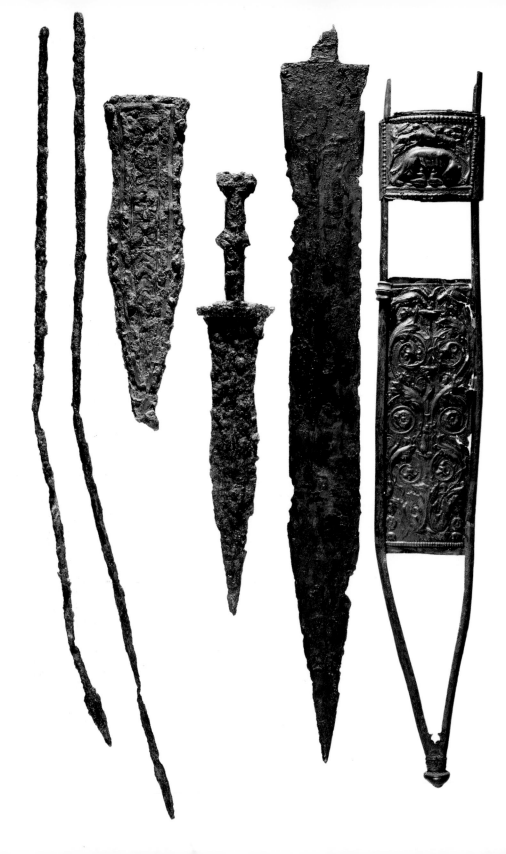

20 OPPOSITE *Legionary weapons, from left to right: two javelin heads, dagger sheath and dagger from Hod Hill, Dorset; and a sword and scabbard from the River Thames at Fulham. At the top of the scabbard, the legendary founders of Rome, Romulus and Remus, are shown being suckled by a she-wolf; 1st century AD.*

constructed in one corner of the hillfort. The types of building discovered, together with the character of the Roman military equipment, demonstrate clearly that detachments of legionary infantry and auxiliary cavalry were brigaded together (figs. 5 and 20). Strategically positioned, Hod Hill was garrisoned for some fifteen years as part of a network of forts and roads with supporting coastal supply bases. These were designed to ensure military control until peaceful conditions allowed transfer of authority to a civilian administration.

By AD 47, conquered territory extended as far north and west as the natural topographic line between Exeter and Lincoln. This line was formalized by the construction of a road, which was to become one of the principal roads of Roman Britain (the 'Fosse Way'), a battle front and line of communication but not a frontier: it marked a pause in

21 BELOW *Small bronze figurine of a virile boar, perhaps from a standard of Legion XX, found at Camerton, Somerset, a probable early fort site on the 'Fosse Way'; 1st century AD.*

22 ABOVE *Spoils of war?*
These tiny bronze figurines
may represent bound
British captives destined
for the slave market;
2nd to 3rd century AD.

campaigning as Aulus Plautius was replaced by the next governor Ostorius Scapula (figs. 5 and 21). With no frontier established and most of the British mineral wealth still in un-conquered territory, much remained to be done. Roads and forts were needed to consolidate gains, together with advanced legionary bases to continue the conquest. But even before that, Scapula had to deal with attacks by hostile tribes who had taken advantage of the lull in activity between governors. Next he turned his attention to the Deceangli tribe of north Wales, which was quickly over-run. But the fierce hill-tribes of Wales, especially the Silures in the south, were a different proposition, and the Roman army was sorely tested by their guerrilla tactics. Nevertheless, in AD 51 the British were defeated in central Wales and Caratacus fled northwards to Cartimandua, queen of the Brigantes. Judging that she could not risk losing Roman support by sheltering Caratacus, she handed him over to the Romans. But resistance continued unabated and, when Scapula died in AD 52, the Silures remained a dauntingly successful enemy. It was already clear that the further conquest of Britain would be a long and costly enterprise, and a succession of governors made only

23 RIGHT *This life-size*
bronze head, hacked from the
statue of an emperor, perhaps
at the time of the Boudican
revolt, used to be identified as
Claudius, but recent research
favours a youthful Nero
(AD 54–68). It was found
in the River Alde at
Rendham, Suffolk.

gradual and sporadic territorial gains. It was to be over thirty years after the invasion before the Welsh tribes and the Brigantes were subdued and garrisoned.

Just how precarious the Roman presence in Britain was came into sharp focus in AD 60, during the reign of Nero (fig. 23). The governor, Suetonius Paullinus, who had arrived in AD 58, rapidly quelled mainland Welsh resistance, and then set his sights on the island of Anglesey. But at his moment of victory, word reached him of a serious rebellion in the heart of the province. Prasutagus, king of the Iceni and a crucial ally, had died. In Roman eyes this signalled the end of the treaty and of the status of the Iceni as people of an independent kingdom. Seemingly with no regard for local sensitivities, an arrogant Roman administration immediately began the process of absorbing the kingdom into the new province. As the Roman historian Tacitus put it, 'Kingdom and household alike were plundered like prizes of war... As a beginning, his widow Boudica was flogged and their daughters raped. The Icenian chiefs were

24 BELOW *An imaginative reconstruction of Boudica's rebels burning the temple of Claudius at Colchester (© Peter Frost/Colchester & Ipswich Museum Service).*

deprived of their hereditary estates as if the Romans had been given the whole country. The king's own relatives were treated like slaves' (Tacitus, *Annals* XIV, 31, about AD 120) (fig. 22). In addition, the neighbouring Trinovantes, already part of the province, had for some time, it seems, suffered badly at the hands of Roman settlers. Deprived of much of the best land, they were nonetheless subjected to high taxation and, to add insult to injury, construction was underway in Colchester of a monumental temple to the deified emperor Claudius, a building that underlined the subjugation of Britain.

History and archaeology combine to provide a vivid, if incomplete, picture of the destruction that followed, including the burning to death of the Roman people of Colchester who had barricaded themselves inside the incomplete temple in the hope of protection (fig. 24). Colchester, St. Albans and London, the main centres of Romans and incomers, were targeted by Boudica, and thick layers of burning, revealed in excavations, confirm the written accounts of Tacitus and Cassius Dio of the sack of these towns. Many of Paullinus' troops were tied to their regions by the general unrest but, fortunately for him, the other southern tribes did not join the rebels. On the brink of losing the province, he cut his losses, leaving London to its fate, and succeeded in forcing a battle, somewhere in the Midlands, between the rebels and his campaigning army — probably no more than 10,000 men. Although the Romans were heavily outnumbered, the rebels were defeated and sustained massive casualties. Boudica committed suicide and the revolt was over. Severe reprisals followed.

In Rome, with reports of the chaos and destruction, it is quite possible that Nero contemplated a retreat from Britain (fig. 25). Instead, control was gradually restored and the decision appears to have been taken to aim for the complete

25 ABOVE *Inlaid-bronze statuette of the emperor Nero (ad 54–68), originally holding a spear or sceptre, and portrayed as a great military leader in the tradition of Alexander the Great; said to be from Barking Hall or Baylham Mill, Suffolk (see also p. 28).*

DIS
MANIBVS
M
CIVLCFF BAITINICLASSICIANI
PROCPROVINCBRITANNIAE
IVLIAINDIELLIAPACATAINDIANA
VXOR F

26 ABOVE *Reconstruction of the stone tomb of Julius Classicianus, who probably died soon after the Boudican revolt of AD 60/61. Set up by his wife in one of Roman London's cemeteries, it was dismantled and re-used in the 4th century (see also fig. 78).*

conquest of the island. An important, perhaps decisive, role in the pacification was played by Julius Alpinus Classicianus, Britain's new finance minister (*procurator*), second only in power to the governor. A provincial himself (from the Rhineland), Classicianus soon realized the futility and damage of Paullinus' reign of terror. With a replacement governor, he set about restoring the province to peace and prosperity, though the archaeological evidence indicates that recovery was a very lengthy process. Underlining the importance of London, Classicianus based himself there, and it was here that he was buried. Remarkably, parts of his tomb were found in 1852 and 1935 (fig. 26).

While a policy of rehabilitation was applied to the restored part of the province, military activity continued in the north, where it was precipitated by internal strife in Cartimandua's Brigantian kingdom. Nevertheless, in AD 67, Nero felt able to remove Legion XIV from Britain, and some ten years later the three principal and enduring legionary bases were established at Caerleon, Chester and York (figs. 5 and 27). With the garrisoning of Wales virtually complete, campaigning was concentrated in northern Britain. The new governor, Julius Agricola, could hardly have been better suited to the task: able, energetic and experienced, he had already completed two tours of duty in Britain, one as an officer on the staff of Suetonius Paullinus, the other as commander of Legion XX (fig. 28). His long governorship (AD 78–84) was both eventful and well-recorded (in the biography written by his son-in-law, Tacitus), and marked the high-point of expansionist policy in Britain. By AD 84, his campaigns had penetrated as far north as the Scottish Highlands, culminating in the battle of Mons Graupius, when a confederacy of Scottish tribes was defeated by Agricola's army, famously composed entirely of auxiliary units with the legions held in reserve.

Construction was started on a

27 BELOW Sandstone altar set up in Chester around AD 100 by the slave household of Titus Pomponius Mamilianus, a commander of Legion XX. It was dedicated to the deities Fortune, Salus and Aesculapius, whose snake-entwined staff, symbol of healing, can be seen on one side.

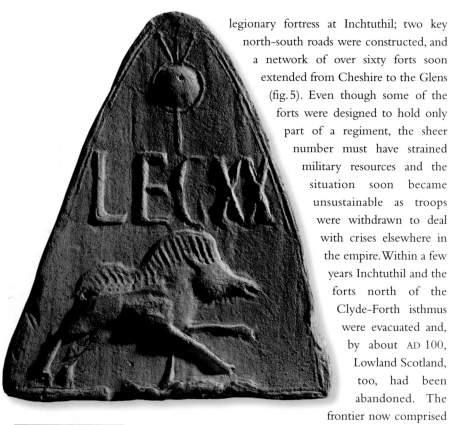

legionary fortress at Inchtuthil; two key north-south roads were constructed, and a network of over sixty forts soon extended from Cheshire to the Glens (fig. 5). Even though some of the forts were designed to hold only part of a regiment, the sheer number must have strained military resources and the situation soon became unsustainable as troops were withdrawn to deal with crises elsewhere in the empire. Within a few years Inchtuthil and the forts north of the Clyde-Forth isthmus were evacuated and, by about AD 100, Lowland Scotland, too, had been abandoned. The frontier now comprised a line of forts and watchtowers connected by a road running from Solway to Tyne, the so-called Stanegate. As Tacitus ruefully observed 'Britain was conquered and immediately let slip' (*Histories*, I, 2, about AD 110).

28 ABOVE Tile plaque with the name and boar emblem of Legion XX, found at the legion's works depot at Holt, near Chester. A line of these plaques would have decorated the eaves of a tiled roof; 2nd to 3rd century AD.

Vindolanda was one of the Stanegate forts, and it is to the period AD 92–115, during the reigns of Domitian, Nerva and Trajan, that the great majority of the Vindolanda writing-Tablets belong. The emperor Hadrian formalized the Solway-Tyne frontier, moving it a short distance forward of the Stanegate forts so that it commanded the high ground. His Wall, about 120 kilometres long, was begun after his visit to Britain in AD 122 (fig. 29). It had a long and complex history, and much remains uncertain, but the original plan appears to have been for a continuous and massive barrier, running from the Tyne at Newcastle to Bowness on the Solway, incorporating regularly-spaced fortlets and towers, with a defensive ditch to the north. Although constructed by contingents from the legions (fig. 30), the main

29 ABOVE *Hadrian's Wall at Housesteads Crags (© Roger Clegg).*

30 RIGHT *Stone inscription from Benwell fort, near the eastern end of Hadrian's Wall, recording building work by Legion II Augusta. It incorporates their legionary standard and emblems, Capricorn (left) and Pegasus (right); 2nd century AD.*

garrison and support troops were initially auxiliary regiments housed in the Stanegate forts. The decision was soon taken, however, to construct sixteen new forts on the line of the wall to enable more rapid deployment of troops. Additionally, the wall was extended both eastwards to Wallsend and westwards down the exposed Cumbrian coast. A road with a continuous linear earthwork behind the Wall demarcated the whole area as a military zone. Ostensibly built 'to separate the barbarians from the Romans', according to Hadrian's biographer Aelius Spartianus (about AD 330), the role of the wall was more likely to divide and control tribal activity on both sides of the frontier. The build-up of hostile forces could be discouraged, the movement of personnel controlled and trade in and out of the province regulated and taxed.

When it was built, Hadrian's Wall was a unique type of frontier in the Roman Empire and, as if to underline that fact, three Roman souvenirs of the wall have survived (fig. 31). They are small, handled pans of bronze inlaid with coloured enamel and inscribed in Latin with the names of some of the forts at the western end of the wall. One has flamboyant Celtic-style ornament and its inscription includes an intriguing phrase – *rigore vali Aeli Draconis* – specifying 'along the line of the Wall' or, perhaps, 'along the line of the Wall of Hadrian', and naming

31 BELOW *Roman souvenir of Hadrian's Wall. This enamelled bronze pan from Ilam, Staffordshire Moorlands, is inscribed with the names of forts at the western end of Hadrian's Wall; 2nd century AD.*

the owner of the pan, Draco, or Aelius Draco, probably a soldier who had the pan made as a reminder of his military service on a remarkable frontier (fig. 31).

The sheer size and complexity of Hadrian's frontier, an extended base for deployment, rather than a sheltered defence, was a huge undertaking involving massive resources – in manpower probably around 15,000 men, for more than ten years. So it is all the more astonishing that, within a few years, in AD 139, under the new emperor Antoninus Pius, the wall was stripped of its garrison, the Scottish Lowlands re-occupied, and the frontier advanced about 130 kilometres north to the line of the Clyde-Forth isthmus (figs. 5 and 32). This shorter frontier (the Antonine Wall), a modified version of Hadrian's Wall, was itself abandoned only a few decades after its completion.

The later second century, especially its final two decades, saw troubled times on Britain's northern frontier, though the written references cannot always be reconciled with the archaeological evidence, and it is clear that military dispositions changed frequently. But after the imperial expedition of Severus and his sons, Caracalla and Geta, and their gruelling campaigns in Scotland (AD 209–11), the frontier returned to Hadrian's Wall, and a long period of (relative) peace ensued.

IV

SOLDIERS AND SOCIETY

'...send me some cash as soon as possible. The hides.... are at Cataractonium.... I would have already been to collect them except that I did not care to injure the animals while the roads are bad. See Tertius about the 8? *denarii*, which he received from Fatalis. He has not credited them to my account...'

Vindolanda Tablet, letter from Octavius to Candidus, about AD 100

LEFT *Decorated bronze boss, from a wooden legionary shield, found near the mouth of the River Tyne; early 2nd century AD (see also fig. 36).*

33 RIGHT *Reconstruction of the equipment of an auxiliary infantryman and cavalry trooper of the mid-1st century AD (illustrated by Karen Hughes).*

THE YEAR AD 43 was the start of a process of profound change. For many Britons, however, it is likely that life did not alter significantly, and the parallel strands of change and continuity are distinctive features of Roman Britain.

The greatest agent of change was the Roman emperor through his provincial administrators, but in practice it was his army that brought the reality of change most forcefully and unequivocally to the native population (fig. 34). However, while such things as the introduction of taxation, Roman law and the use of Latin were inescapable, many existing customs, whether farming methods, land tenure, religious practice or art styles, continued little changed alongside, or integrated with, new ways. Certainly, in the scattered farms and settlements of the northern and western parts of the province, the impact of Roman material culture appears to have been much weaker. There, the bastions of Roman culture were not towns, of which there were only a handful, but the forts and fortresses of the Roman garrison, centres not just of control and ever-present potential violence, but of spending-power and Romanized customs, drawn from all corners of the empire and overlain with a distinct military identity.

It has been suggested that very little of the surviving remains of Roman Britain, whether artefacts or buildings, do not owe their existence directly or indirectly to the army. Put another way, if we subtract the 'military material' from the archaeology of Roman Britain, we are left with comparatively little evidence of Roman culture. This is hardly surprising, given the fact

34 LEFT *Reconstruction of the equipment of a legionary soldier of the later 1st century AD (illustrated by R. Pengelly).*

35 RIGHT *Tombstone from Lincoln of Gaius Saufeius, a soldier from Heraclea in Macedonia, who served in Legion IX Hispana, and died in the AD sixties, aged forty, after twenty-two years' service.*

that Britain was top-heavy with armed forces. With a complement of three legions and a correspondingly large number of auxiliary units for most of the period of Roman rule, Britain differed markedly from most other provinces, where the military presence was far smaller. Such a concentration of troops for such a long period is only partly explained by the strength of resistance to Roman rule. It may be that, as a remote island at the very edge of the empire, Britain was regarded as a convenient place to isolate legions, perhaps when an emperor's authority was threatened. However, the explanation may be more mundane, for the reign of Hadrian marked an end to imperial expansion after which, partly through simple inertia, garrisons tended to remain in their provinces, being mobilized only in times of crisis. Whatever the case, this concentration of troops was a permanent and substantial drain on Britain's resources.

Britain's garrison combined both legionary and auxiliary troops. In the first two centuries AD, the legions were the backbone of the Roman army. Each consisted of some 5,000 crack infantry – heavily armed, highly trained and strictly disciplined (fig. 34). Recruits were Roman citizens from throughout the empire, who satisfied health and stature requirements and signed up, normally around the age of eighteen to twenty, for a period of twenty-five years (fig. 35). Training was tough, but high pay-rates, good promotion prospects and a substantial grant of land or money on

36 ABOVE *Bronze shield boss from the river Tyne inscribed and decorated with the name and bull emblem of Legion VIII Augusta, part of which served in Britain under the emperor Hadrian (AD 117–138); (see also fig. 37 below).*

retirement ensured a constant supply of recruits. Each legion was commanded by a general, a man of senatorial rank, usually in his early thirties, selected by the emperor himself. He was supported by six junior officers, but the most experienced and battle-hardened soldiers in the legion were the sixty centurions, each of whom led a 'century' of eighty men. They directed the soldiers on the battlefield and usually determined the outcome of the battle. Experience and responsibility were reflected in their pay – about twenty times that of the ordinary legionary. Others, too, had the opportunity to increase their status and pay, for the complex legionary hierarchy included many men with special skills or duties, like metalsmiths, clerks, standard-bearers, musicians and doctors. The first rung on the promotion ladder was immunity from unpleasant duties, from which a soldier could progress first to a one-and-a-half-times' pay-rate and then to double pay.

The most distinctive items of legionary equipment were the

heavy javelin (*pilum*) (fig. 20), and curved rectangular shield (*scutum*) (fig. 36). Equally distinctive, though not exclusive to the legions were the dagger (*pugio*), the short-bladed thrusting sword (*gladius*) and segmented armour (fig. 34). This type of armour was developed in the first century AD and provided effective protection against slashing blows from long swords. Various types of helmet were worn, either of bronze or iron or a combination of the two (figs. 33, 38). Common to all helmets were domed bowls with hinged cheek-pieces and an integral neckguard, which protected the head, neck and shoulders, while the brow-guard was designed to deflect downward-slashing sword-blows from the face. Soldiers were issued with their arms and equipment, which had to be returned to stores at the end of their service. Some soldiers marked their name on individual pieces, presumably to avoid loss or theft (fig. 37). It seems that individuality could also be expressed by commissioning decorative parts for certain items, such as sword and dagger scabbards, helmets or shield coverings (fig. 39).

Serving alongside and supplementing the heavy infantry of the legions were regiments of non-citizen auxilia ('aids'), mostly about 500 strong, who provided principally light infantry and cavalry, but also included specialists, most notably archers, slingers and those who could swim in full kit. A small but significant contingent were the marine units of the British fleet (*classis Britannica*), an arm of the Roman navy, created in

37 **BELOW** *Detail of fig. 36 showing the left side of the shield boss with the dot-punched ownership inscription of Junius Dubitatus, a soldier in Legion VIII Augusta.*

38 LEFT *Legionary bronze helmet from London, with a cheek-protector and plume-holder at the side, a brow-guard at the front, a broad-flanged neck-protector at the back and a crest-holder at the top; 1st century AD.*

39 ABOVE *Bronze helmet with British-style decoration on the broad neck-guard. Said to have been found in the north of England, it was probably made for a Roman auxiliary soldier during the 1st century AD.*

preparation for the invasion of Britain. With its principal base at Dover, the fleet operated in close support with the Roman land forces, both as a raiding force and as a key part of the military supply system. Agricola's campaigns in northern Scotland were heavily dependent on naval support and intelligence reports, and parts of the fleet rounded, explored and mapped the coasts of Scotland and Ireland. The fleet returned to prominence in the third century, when the south and east coasts, in particular, were under threat (see chapter IX).

Auxiliary units, initially used as scouts and flank-guards on campaign, and for routine patrolling and defence, soon joined the legions in the forefront of battle (fig. 33). The infantry regiments (*cohortes peditatae*) were always more numerous than the expensive wings (*alae*) of cavalry, but mixed units of infantry and cavalry (*cohortes equitatae*) proved highly versatile and became increasingly popular. In AD 122, when Hadrian came to Britain, the auxiliary force consisted of fourteen *alae* and about forty-seven *cohortes*, of which seven were double-size units, a total of about 35,000

40 LEFT *Bronze figurine from London depicting one of the North African Moorish cavalrymen, who were famed for nimble horsemanship. Originally seated on a horse, he has distinctive dreadlocks, silver inlaid eyes and a round shield.*

men. The *alae* were the most prestigious auxiliary units, though still ranked lower than the legions, and were of particular importance because the legions themselves had no combatant cavalry. Their mobility often gave them a crucial role at the height of a battle, and they were frequently used, too, to underscore a victory by pursuing and harassing a defeated enemy (figs. 12 and 40).

Auxiliary soldiers were normally recruited from new provinces or from tribes outside the empire, and their dress and equipment sometimes reflected their origins (fig. 40). Usually, however, during the first to third centuries AD, they wore an armoured tunic of iron mail, or bronze scales, and carried a flat oval shield (fig. 33). Their swords tended to be longer than the legionary *gladius*, and spears differed according to unit, the narrow-bladed lance being well-adapted to cavalry use. However, much of the success of the Roman army came from its

41 ABOVE *Bronze 'diploma' from Malpas, Cheshire, issued in AD 103 by the emperor Trajan (AD 98–117). It certified the rights to citizenship and legal marriage of Reburrus, a junior cavalry officer of Spanish origin, who had served in Britain.*

ability to adapt to face different enemies. Accordingly, the type of equipment and the composition of units were constantly evolving. On completion of twenty-five years' service, auxiliary soldiers were granted citizenship for themselves and their children, as well as the right to legal marriage. These precious rights allowed a soldier to raise considerably both his own status and that of his family, and he received his own copy of his new rights in the form of a pair of inscribed bronze plates, like those of the cavalryman Reburrus (fig. 41).

In combat, the complementary roles of legionaries and auxiliaries were used to devastating effect against opposing forces. Similarly, their non-combat duties in peacetime differed in order to maximize resources. Routine patrols and policing were generally carried out by the auxiliaries, and large construction projects by legionaries. At all events, when active campaigning was not in progress, it was critical to ensure that all troops were fully occupied because they were expensive to maintain and those in power always feared that soldiers with time on their hands might more readily be led astray.

The primary concern was with training, exercise and manoeuvres, described in military texts and confirmed by the discovery of parade grounds, practice camps and amphitheatres outside many forts and fortresses, as at Caerleon, Chester, Maryport, South Shields and Hardknott (fig. 42). Weapons drill and marching practice were the mainstay of infantry training while cavalry units required constant attention to keep them at the peak of fitness and effectiveness. Regular parades allowed commanding officers to review their troops. Perhaps the most spectacular occasions were the cavalry sports events (*hippika gymnasia*), flamboyant displays of military horsemanship and mounted weapons drill, combining discipline and split-second timing (figs. 43–44). They culminated in mock battles between the elite riders of the unit, usually in the guise of Greeks and Amazons, wearing elaborate suites of parade equipment.

Initially, the legions were employed on large-scale building projects, since they combined a large controllable work-force with many different specialists – architects, engineers, land-surveyors, masons, carpenters and blacksmiths. Their prime concern was with their own massive fortresses, the *coloniae* of retired legionaries (see chapter VII), frontiers, roads and communications infrastructure. Soon, however, the construction and maintenance work was shared by auxiliaries. Fort and fortress alike had a workshop (*fabrica*) where weapons and equipment could be repaired. For more specialized or larger-scale maintenance and manufacture, including pottery and tile production, works depots were required, as at Corbridge, Holt (near Chester) and Walton-le-Dale (fig. 28).

Self-sufficiency was a logical policy for the military in Britain, as elsewhere, but there was also considerable contact and collaboration with parts of the civilian population, whether the

43 BELOW *Reconstruction of two cavalry troopers preparing for the* hippika gymnasia *(cavalry sports) around the year AD 100. The equipment of the horse and soldier to the right is based on objects in the hoard from Ribchester, Lancashire (see fig. 44) (illustrated by Karen Hughes).*

44 Hoard of military equipment, probably the possessions of a single cavalryman, from Ribchester, Lancashire. Buried around AD 120, it was found by a clog-maker's son in 1796.

THE RIBCHESTER HELMET, *a two-piece embossed brass vizor helmet consisting of a peaked head-piece and a hinged face-mask, secured at the neck with leather straps. This is one of the finest examples of the helmets worn by top cavalrymen in the colourful displays known as cavalry sports (hippika gymnasia). Appropriately, the scene on the head-piece (above) depicts a skirmish between cavalry and infantry.*

EYE-GUARDS *These strange-looking objects protected a horse's eyes in battle. Made of pierced bronze, they were attached to decorated leather chamfrons, which encased the front of the horse's head; both horse and rider were masked (see the reconstruction above).*

HORSE BRASS *A set of richly-decorated harness ornaments consisting of silver-plated discs, saddle plates and pendants (see the reconstruction below and opposite).*

BATH SAUCERS *Two shallow bronze pans used for dousing the body with water at the baths.*

MORTARIUM *A pottery mixing bowl with a gritted surface, widely used in the preparation of Roman-style dishes.*

SAUCEPAN (MESS-TIN) *of bronze (broken) for the preparation of meals, part of the standard military issue to Roman soldiers.*

TUSK *of a wild boar, symbol of ferocity and virility, perhaps a hunting trophy originally mounted and worn by the cavalryman as a good-luck amulet.*

45 ABOVE *Lead ingot, from Hints Common, Staffordshire, weighing 68.27 kg. The inscriptions name the emperors Vespasian and Titus, date the ingot to* AD *76 and indicate that the lead came from the territory of the Deceangli in north-east Wales.*

securing of provisions for the army, assistance with civic building projects or regional administration. The great forum-basilica complexes and baths at places like London, St. Albans, Wroxeter and Leicester may have drawn on the architectural and management skills of military personnel, even if the initiative came from the town council. The army also helped with administration, supervising, for example, the mining and transport of metals, on which the Roman state had a monopoly (fig. 45). Certainly no time was lost in activating extraction and, even while campaigning was in progress, exploitation of the lead ore *galena* was underway in the Mendips by AD 49, after which control was handled by the *procurator*. Lead from the Mendips, North Wales and Derbyshire was used extensively as a waterproofing agent for roof-flashing, the lining of baths and the manufacture of pipes and tanks. Metal ingots, whether of silver, lead or copper, were marked with official inscriptions, often with countermarks, to control their circulation. At Dolaucothi, near Pumpsaint, Dyfed in Wales, the mining of gold was closely supervised by a military unit in garrison at the adjacent fort (figs. 5 and 46). Even iron production was in some areas controlled by the military, as in the Weald of Kent, where detachments of the British Fleet (*classis Britannica*) appear to have been involved.

While textual and archaeological evidence have shed light on the activities of the army and occasionally on that of individuals, the discovery of the Vindolanda Tablets has provided a vivid glimpse of everyday life and the personal aspirations of soldiers at both work and leisure (see chapter v). Fragmentary as many of them are, the sheer variety and detail of the letters and documents are simply astonishing (figs. 60–1). The ink writing-tablets, which owe their survival to burial in waterlogged ground, are wafer-thin slices of wood (mainly birch and alder) with texts written in carbon ink using quill-type pens (fig. 47). Unknown before their discovery at Vindolanda in 1973, such tablets have since been found at other sites in Britain, most notably Carlisle, but so far only in much smaller numbers. Nevertheless, they would appear to have been widespread in both Britain and probably some of the north-west provinces, where previously it was thought that the commonest 'stationery' was waxed stilus-tablets and papyrus (fig. 53). Most of the tablets are official documents relating to the occupation of the fort by successive auxiliary regiments. There are lists, memoranda, reports, leave requests and accounts, shedding light on unit strength, military routine and duties, secondment of staff, transport and medicine, cash transactions and the provision and distribution of a wide range of food supplies, clothing and equipment.

Of great importance, and the first of its kind from Britain, is a military document detailing the strength of the unit in garrison at Vindolanda around the years AD 92–7, the First Cohort of Tungrians. This was a double-size regiment, recruited in northern Gaul, with a nominal total of 800 men. The tablet shows that it was close to its full complement, though four centurions short of the normal ten. However, of the 752 soldiers on the roll, only 296 were present at Vindolanda, of whom just 265 were fit for active service, the remainder being sick or wounded. Of the absentees, the great majority were a single detachment of 337 on a tour of duty at nearby Corbridge (*Coria*), while a further forty-six were detached for duty as guards with the governor of the province and assigned to a man named Ferox, who may have been the commander of Legion IX Hispana at York. The text on this single sliver of wood is a salutary reminder of the complexities of military logistics that are usually lost to us.

46 BELOW *Gem-set, enamelled and filigree gold jewellery, comprising a finger-ring, hinged bracelet and neck ornament. Found in Rhayader, Powys, Wales, it was made during the 1st or 2nd century AD.*

Another novelty, which sheds new light on the day-to-day military routine, are several examples of a previously unknown type of document headed *renuntium* ('report'). These appear to be checks on personnel and equipment – a sort of 'all present and correct' report – made at regular intervals and submitted to the deputy centurions (*optiones*). Perhaps the most memorable of the military documents, however, is a tantalizing fragment of what appears to be a report discussing the suitability of locals for military service. For the writer describes them as *Brittunculi*, a disparaging term which translates as 'Little Brits', indicating a rather patronizing, if not contemptuous, Roman military regime.

Many other tablets, though, are private letters sent to, or occasionally drafted by, the serving soldiers and officers. We read of hopes for promotion, requests for letters of recommendation, and meetings scheduled with high officials, including the provincial governor. Famously, in several letters, officers' wives arrange a birthday party (figs. 60–1) and discuss illness; while elsewhere ordinary soldiers write home requesting socks and underpants, or scold fellow soldiers for failing to reply to letters. In the largest and most complete text – an unpretentious business letter folded before the ink was dry – we hear of

48 RIGHT *Bronze statuette of the god Mars from Fossdyke, Torksey, Lincolnshire. The unusually detailed inscription on the base names the dedicators, Bruccius and Caratius, the maker, Celatus and the costs involved in manufacture; 1st to 3rd century AD.*

the supply of goods on a huge scale interspersed with frequent references to large sums of cash (fig. 47). We also learn of some of the ways that individuals spent their spare time and some of the entertainment they enjoyed. While soldiers asked for leave to visit the 'bright lights' of nearby *Coria* and bought themselves extra rations or luxuries for the many religious festivals, officers requested more beer for their men or corresponded about hounds, nets and snares for hunting, a pastime much enjoyed by those who had the opportunity (see chapter VII).

Disconcertingly, and a reminder of the brutality that could erupt at any moment, one civilian writer, 'a citizen, from overseas', seeks redress from those in authority – perhaps from the governor himself – for an unwarranted beating that he has suffered. Together, the Vindolanda Tablets give a fascinating insight into the wide range of peacetime duties and activities of an auxiliary regiment and of the sheer scale of 'paperwork' generated by the Roman army in Britain.

Hunting, religious practice and liaisons with women in the garrison settlements are some of the activities also attested by other archaeological finds, whether inscribed stone altars or statuettes dedicated to Mars, Jupiter, Mithras or other gods with particular appeal to the military (fig. 48); amulets, like the boar's tusk found with the Ribchester parade equipment (fig. 44); or tombstones set up by or to wives and children (figs. 49–50). Certainly, for those soldiers who survived to complete their period of service, the army provided security, paid them well and looked after their health

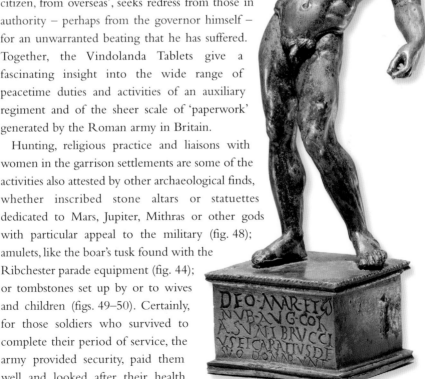

and fitness. In retirement some may have returned to their birthplace, moved to another province, set up home or business in one of Britain's towns or, perhaps, bought an estate or farm, but many probably made only the very short move to an adjacent or nearby garrison settlement, a military community in which they felt at home. The garrison settlements varied greatly in size and status, from the substantial and relatively sophisticated legionary *canabae* at Caerleon, Chester and York to the more modest *vici* and smaller places outside auxiliary forts – but most shared a similar mix of inhabitants, united by being part of a military community: veterans, citizens, civilians and slaves, merchants, traders, soldiers' children (fig. 49), wives, common-law wives, sexual partners and prostitutes. Legionaries, especially, began their retirement with considerable wealth and status, based on a grant of land or a substantial cash settlement. However they fared, these veterans were at least assured a proper burial through membership of a military burial club (*collegium*), financed by compulsory deductions from pay while in service. Although a tombstone was not included – that was the duty of the heirs – the burial itself and a funeral feast were covered. Such gatherings, doubtless a regular part of the social life of the garrison settlements, must have echoed to incantations, song and conversation in several different languages, as those of British, Germanic and Gallic extraction mingled with people from other parts of Europe, the Middle East and North Africa (fig. 50).

49 LEFT *Tombstone from Old Penrith, Cumbria, set up for Marcus Cocceius Nonnus, who died aged six during the early 2nd century AD. The boy is shown with the whip and palm-branch of a victorious charioteer, Roman symbols of victory over death.*

50 RIGHT *Tombstone, from Lincoln, of Titus Valerius Pudens, a soldier from Savaria (modern Hungary), who died aged thirty, after six years' service in Legion II Adiutrix during the 1st century AD.*

T·VALERIVS·T·F
CLA·PVDENS·SAV
MIL·LEG·II·A·P·F·
⊃ DOSSENN·⸱
PROCVLI·A·XX
AIK   L·D·S·P
H·S·E·

V

LANGUAGE AND LITERACY

'[Agricola] began to train the sons of the chieftains in a liberal education…. As a result, the nation which used to reject the Latin language began to aspire to rhetoric. Further, …. the toga came into fashion, …. the promenade, the bath, the well-appointed dinner table.'

Tacitus, *Agricola*, XXI, 2, AD 98

LEFT *Birthday invitation to Sulpicia Lepidina, about* AD *100. Wooden writing-tablet, Vindolanda, Northumberland (see also fig. 60).*

FROM THE MOMENT ROMAN SOLDIERS set foot in Britain prehistory turned into history. The Celtic languages of Iron Age Britain were spoken not written and the few remnants of writing to have survived from before the conquest are mostly names written in Latin or Greek letters adapted to use on British coins (fig. 15).

Some native Britons before the conquest may have been literate in Latin, and some possibly even 'educated' in Rome. Latin was to remain the official language of Britain for the four centuries of Roman rule. It was the language of Roman society in the western provinces of the empire, and of law, administration and business. For all who had dealings with the Roman administration, it would have been necessary both to understand and speak Latin and for some it may have been essential, beneficial or desirable both to read and write the language (fig. 51).

It is impossible to tell how many people in Britain were literate in Latin or to gauge precisely the numbers or percentages of the degree of literacy, but we can at least assume a sliding scale from understanding and speaking to reading and writing. We can certainly anticipate a basic knowledge of the spoken language, even of those who did not read or write, through contact with the army administrative and judicial systems.

But what do we mean by literacy anyway? Today in the developed

51 RIGHT *Bronze saucepan from Prickwillow, Cambridgeshire. The name of the maker, BODVOGENVS, recalling the British Celtic names Bodvoc and Boudica, is stamped near the end of the ornate handle; 2nd century AD.*

world, illiteracy has very negative connotations. But how might we compare a person who speaks, reads and writes in just one language, with a person who understands and speaks several but reads and writes in none? Late Iron Age society in Britain was not necessarily unsophisticated for the virtual absence of literacy, merely different. Once Britain became a province of Rome, however, literacy in Latin was critical for those seeking, or seeking to retain, positions of power and influence. However, Latin and British were not the only languages to be heard, for the Roman Empire united many different cultures through trade, military service and the administration of government. Even in the towns and forts of a distant province like Britain the ethnic mix included people from all parts of the empire, each speaking their own language in

52 ABOVE *Small bronze oil flask for use at the baths, decorated with three Black African heads. It was found with other bath accessories in a burial at Bayford, Kent; 2nd century AD.*

53 A selection of objects for writing in ink and on wax, from various sites in Roman London, 1st to 2nd century AD.

INK WELL *of brown-coated pottery with a non-spill rim, inscribed in Latin with the personal name IVCVNDI, meaning 'Property of Iucundus'. The ink it would have contained was made from gum, soot and water, rather like our 'Indian' ink, and was probably traded and stored in powdered form to be mixed with water when needed.*

PENS *Two tubular bronze dip-pens with split nibs, for writing in ink on papyrus or on wooden leaf-tablets, like those from the fort at Vindolanda. Simpler, cheaper pens made from reeds or quills (feathers) were probably more common than those of metal, but have not survived.*

WRITING EQUIPMENT 1ST–2ND CENTURY AD

STILUS-TABLETS, *wooden writing tablets preserved in water-logged conditions, which inhibited the normal process of decay. Their inner face was recessed to take a wax coating into which letters and documents were written using the pointed tip of a stilus.*

IRON STILUS *for writing on the waxed surface of wooden stilus-tablets. Like the bronze stilus (below), it has a pointed writing tip, slender grip and wedge-shaped eraser. Made of iron, it is stamped with the name of its maker, Regnus.*

STATIONERY *The outside of this government stilus-tablet bears an official brand in abbreviated Latin:* PROC AVG DEDERVNT BRIT PROV: *'Issued by the Imperial Procurators (finance ministers) of the Province of Britain'.*

BRONZE-GRIP STILUS, *possibly more costly than the iron stilus (top), it combines a hard-wearing iron nib with a highly-decorated bronze grip.*

LETTER FRAGMENT *The letter's writer, Rufus, pressed so hard with his stilus that it penetrated the wax, and preserved a tantalizing part of his message in the underlying wood. He asks Epillicus to send a list, and instructs him to 'extract the last coin from that girl'.*

addition to Latin (fig. 52). Some left written evidence, such as an altar in Cumbria dedicated by a Mauretanian, a tombstone from South Shields set up by a Syrian, a religious vow in Colchester made by a Caledonian and correspondence from Vindolanda between two Greek brothers. Such diversity reinforced the importance of Latin as a common language.

Although language and literacy were fundamental to all aspects of daily life, our knowledge of them in Roman Britain is sparse, and no works of any famous literary figures from Roman Britain have survived. The archaeological sources for literacy combine indirect evidence – writing implements – with the direct evidence of the texts themselves. Two types of written Latin would almost immediately have confronted people. Capital-letter texts were inscribed on grand buildings, above fort and town gateways, on statue bases, altars and tombstones, but they were also present on a smaller scale on coins, which brought the emperor's image, his propaganda and writing to almost all levels of society. The principal script for letters and documents, necessarily more flowing than capitals, is known as cursive. That it continued to evolve over the period of Roman rule in Britain is apparent from two important sources of handwritten texts in the province, the Vindolanda Tablets and the lead curses from Bath and Uley.

54 BELOW The power of the written word: a tiny bronze box exquisitely inlaid with miniature panels of coloured enamel (millefiori). It was probably a high-status ink-well; 2nd century AD.

Writing implements comprised ink-wells, pens, stili and seal-boxes (fig. 53). The few surviving pens are slender tubes of bronze with a pointed split-nib, but the most common are likely to have been reed or quill pens. The use of such pens is at least confirmed by their distinctive script seen in many of the texts on the Vindolanda Tablets. The ink used was carbon ink, a mixture of gum-water and soot. Ink-wells for these dip-pens are similarly sparse in Britain, although examples made in glossy red Samian ware imported from Gaul have been found in quite large numbers in London. More

prestigious were examples of bronze, often decorated with costly inlays (fig. 54). Stili were used to write on wooden tablets with a waxed surface – small rectangular boards with a central recessed panel filled with wax, into which writing was incised (fig. 53). Often they consisted of a facing pair tied together, but, when necessary, several tablets could be strung together. Even when waterlogged conditions have preserved the wooden tablet, the wax seldom survives, but sometimes the writer pressed so hard that the text was cut into the wood backing, making it occasionally possible to decipher. A famous example from London appears to concern an inventory and financial matters, ending with the enigmatic phrase 'See that you do everything carefully so as to extract the last coin from that girl....' A more complete text on another London tablet, dated 14 March 118, is the first page of a legal document concerning the contested ownership of a wood in Kent. That stilus-tablets were often selected for

legal texts is also suggested by an example from Trawsfynydd, North Wales – the first page of a very long will, probably that of a retired auxiliary soldier who had settled and bought land in the region.

Virtually all surviving stili are of bronze or iron, but bone examples are known and many more must have been made of wood. They are thin pencil-like rods with a solid pointed writing tip at one end and a wedge-shaped eraser at the other. Interestingly, the common and wide distribution of stili in Britain includes many 'lower-status' settlements, perhaps suggesting that literacy was not confined to any one social group. Stili were probably used also to write the texts on lead 'curses' and on religious plaques. In the absence of the texts themselves, small bronze seal-boxes, like stili, hint at the existence of literacy in the places where they are found. To ensure their confidentiality, letters and documents were tied with string, which was then passed through holes in a seal-box into which molten wax was poured, cooled, and impressed with the sender's seal. The seal-box's hinged lid protected the wax until the recipient broke the seal.

Most enduring of the direct evidence for writing are inscriptions cut in stone (fig. 56). They range from monumental building inscriptions set up to celebrate the completion of grand projects like forum-basilica complexes in towns, or the construction of forts and fortresses, to diminutive inscribed stone stamps used for marking eye-medicines. Some of the grander inscriptions, like that on the tomb of the *procurator* Julius Classicianus (fig. 26), are top-quality, sophisticated works with exquisitely cut letters aesthetically arranged and even provided with accents. Picked out in red paint, these inscriptions were designed to impress the viewer and be pleasing in

56 LEFT *Milestone from Llanfairfechan, Gwynedd, Wales, erected in* AD *120–1. The inscription, originally picked out in red paint, proclaims the imperial powers of Hadrian, and records a distance of 8 miles (13 kilometres) to the Roman fort of Canovium (Caerhun).*

their appearance, but first and foremost they were imperial propaganda, naming the emperor, underlining his authority and power and only then naming his agent, for instance the governor, who had been responsible for the construction. Such inscriptions shed light on military and administrative matters and are often valuable for dating the building work.

Epitaphs on tombstones, on the other hand, are more informative of individuals, though most are prosaic (fig. 57). Name, family and heirs, birth-place or home town and age at death are briefly recorded, sometimes with a short phrase of endearment, such as 'to his well-deserving wife'. Soldiers' tombstones and those of officers and administrators usually provide details of careers, naming the military unit, position and period of service, or listing official postings in chronological order, while civilians might proclaim their citizenship or state their membership of a town council or priesthood of the imperial cult (figs. 35, 50 and 58). At South Shields, Barates, a native of Palmyra (Syria), set up a fine tombstone to Regina, a slave-girl from the St. Albans region, whom he had bought, freed and married. The main inscription is in Latin but a brief tender epitaph is also written in Palmyrene.

Stone altars, for use at religious sites or in cult rooms in forts, were usually gifts by the moderately wealthy, for example, military officers or merchants. When inscribed, they often name just the deity, dedicator and his or her status as, for example, an altar found in the Saxon-shore fort at Lympne, Kent, dedicated to the sea-god

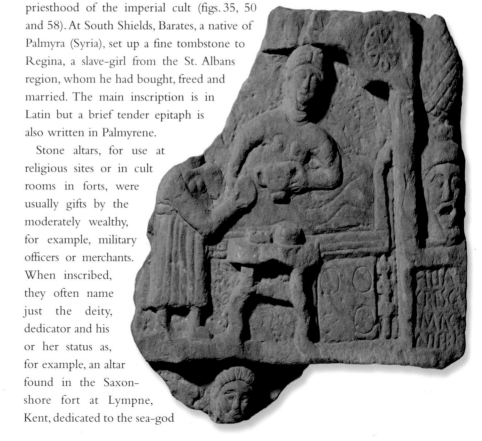

57 BELOW *Broken tombstone of the daughter of a military standard-bearer named Crescens. Erected in Kirkby Thore, Cumbria, from the 2nd to 4th century AD, the tombstone relief shows a 'funeral banquet', with the deceased woman being served as she reclines on a couch.*

58 LEFT *Tombstone of Volusia Faustina and Claudia Catiotua. Faustina was the wife of Aurelius Senecio, a town councillor of* Lindum *(Lincoln), where the tombstone was erected during the 3rd century AD. Claudia may have been her mother or Senecio's second wife.*

Neptune by a commander of the British Fleet. An optimistic dedication on another altar, from the fort at Maryport, Cumbria was designed to cover all eventualities by naming a consortium of deities – the Spirit of the Place, Fortune the Home-bringer, Eternal Rome and Good Fate. The dedicator was a military officer named Gaius Cornelius Peregrinus, formerly a town councillor at *Saldae* in North Africa (fig. 59).

Sometimes altars were gifts to a deity, like one found at Bordeaux, which had been dedicated to Tutela Boudiga – a British version of the Roman goddess Victory – by Marcus Aurelius Lunaris, a merchant, 'in fulfilment of a vow that he had made when he set out from *Eburacum* [York]'. Sea-voyages, especially with valuable cargo, were risky and needed divine protection.

Vows to deities were also fulfilled through the gift of decorative metal plaques, of gold, silver or bronze, to be displayed in temple buildings. When inscribed groups of such gifts are found, they give an insight into religious practice, for example by revealing the range of devotees: at Ashwell, Hertfordshire, the goddess Senuna appears to have had a particular appeal for women (fig. 104). The contractual nature of human relationships with pagan gods and goddesses affected even the practice of early Christianity in Britain, as evidenced by the silver plaques in the Water Newton hoard of Church plate, which include one given by Anicilla in fulfilment of a vow (fig. 108). Like the inscriptions in the Ashwell temple treasure, those at Water Newton reveal a few details about a religious community; similarly, members of another group, perhaps a

59 RIGHT *Sandstone altar, found in 1587 at the fort of Maryport, Cumbria. The dedicator, Peregrinus, may have been yearning for his home town,* Saldae *(Bejaia, Algeria), for he included Fortune, the Home-bringer, in his list of deities.*

guild, inscribed their names on the underside of a Samian bowl, from Ospringe in Kent, which they described as a 'communal vessel'. Such scratched graffiti are found in great quantity on pottery vessels, usually just a name or symbol indicating ownership, but sometimes a weight or capacity.

Such individual finds permit glimpses of literacy, but there are two complementary groups of written material that provide a much richer resource for the study of literacy in Roman Britain: first, the Vindolanda wooden writing-tablets, already touched on in the context of army life (see chapter IV); and, second, the lead curses from Bath and Uley. The Vindolanda Tablets, concerning the affairs of a military community on the northern frontier in the decades around the year AD 100, are very different to the curses found at the temples of Sulis Minerva at Bath, and Mercury at Uley, both of which reflect the concerns of part of the province's civilian population from the second to fourth century AD. The combination of these two resources does not give a complete picture, but offers vivid examples of the power of the written word in particular places, at particular times, by certain groups and individuals.

Although we have already sampled the intriguing details of military activity disclosed by the Vindolanda Tablets (figs. 60–1), they reveal much more besides. Perhaps most striking of all – apart from their fascinating content – is the sheer variety of individual handwriting. The tablets were written by several hundred people, scribes, senior and junior officers, soldiers and women alike. If, as is probable, they represent the tip of an iceberg, they indicate a greater and wider level of literacy in Britain, at least in the military community, than had previously been suspected. They also demonstrate the way in which letters and documents were written. Most of the larger tablets are roughly the size of a postcard, and the smallest ones about half that. The letters were generally written with the broad dimension of the leaf running horizontally and the text set out in two columns, the first at the left; the second at the right (fig. 60). After completing the letter, the writer scored it vertically down the centre, folded it, and wrote the address on the back of the right-hand half. Some tablets had notches cut into the edge so that they could be tied together. The military reports and accounts were often written with the text running across the grain and parallel to the short edge of the tablet. This format lent itself well to the compiling of lists, and in some cases several of the leaves were joined together in a concertina format to form a wooden notebook.

Accounting practices are revealed and also the use of

61 BELOW *Detail of the letter in fig. 60 (opposite), showing Claudia Severa's own closing words at the end of the second column – some of the earliest surviving handwriting in Latin by a woman.*

shorthand writing involving a combination of letters and symbols. Several tablets are re-used, with drafts or writing-practice on the reverse. Of particular interest is a line from Virgil's *Aeneid* (written about a century earlier in the twenties BC), probably copied out as a writing exercise, perhaps even by a child of Flavius Cerealis, one of Vindolanda's unit commanders. Virgil was extensively used for elementary instruction but it is interesting to find knowledge of his work so far north. In fact, there is wider evidence for knowledge of his writings in several parts of Britain. Two Virgilian inscriptions survive in villas in Kent. One is a fragmentary painted phrase, part of an inscribed frieze of scenes from the *Aeneid*, which decorated a corridor wall in a villa at Otford. The other appears on a floor mosaic in the dining-room at Lullingstone villa: bordering a scene of Jupiter abducting Europa is a clever Latin verse intended to recall the episode as described in the *Aeneid*. Both inscriptions reflect the Romanized literary tastes of the villas' owners.

A far-cry, perhaps, from refined dinner-parties in late fourth-century Kent are the messages incised on small sheets of lead, so-called curses, known in antiquity as *defixiones*. Individual examples are known from various sites, mostly in south-west Britain, and large quantities were consigned to the sacred spring of Sulis Minerva at Bath and to the god Mercury in a rural sanctuary at Uley, Gloucestershire (figs. 5 and 62). The curses are more correctly petitions to a god, not spells, but appeals for justice to the highest authority. Concerned principally with theft, the language is very uniform and formulaic and is believed not only to reflect spoken Latin, but also the influence of the Celtic language: about half the names are Celtic, and bilingualism is even hinted at by a few texts, which may be spoken Celtic transcribed into Latin. Lead sheet, cheap, easily made and readily inscribed, was accessible to most; and study of the names indicates that generally the petitioners were not citizens but people of local origin, often at the lower end of the social scale. The texts, probably written mostly by the petitioners themselves, perhaps with advice from priests, generally sought to enlist the aid of the god(s) in restoring stolen property or in inflicting harm on wrong-doers (fig. 63). Theft of clothing ('that he exact vengeance for the gloves') or agricultural stock ('I have lost two wheels and four cows') are frequently cited. Sometimes the curses were given extra power by reversing the writing or by nailing the curse to a wall, while at Uley they were generally rolled up. Their set formulae ('whether man or woman, whether boy or girl, whether slave

62 RIGHT *Coarse stone, but a fine sculpture: the over-lifesize limestone head of the cult statue of Mercury. It was found in his sanctuary at Uley, Gloucestershire; 2nd century AD.*

or free'), quasi-legal phraseology ('the aforesaid property to the aforesaid temple') and sometimes vindictive, or gruesome imprecations ('that you drive them to the greatest death and do not allow them health or sleep', 'may he be accursed in his blood and eyes and every limb, or even have all his guts eaten away'), make startling reading, but the central messages give us unique access to part of the seedier side of Romano-British society and the real concerns of people in their daily life.

Less alarming, perhaps, are the more positive, if sometimes rather mystifying, magical texts of protective amulets, incised on lead sheets or gold leaf, a few of which have been found in Britain (fig. 64). Concentrating power by combining a Latin or Greek text with magical symbols and invocations to gods, such amulets were believed to protect the wearer from evil. Some are generic talismans 'for protection', but others have a specific role 'for health and victory' or safe childbirth. All are united in their attempt to harness power through language, and, like the lead curses and wooden writing-tablets, they illustrate the degree to which language and literacy permeated all levels of society.

63 LEFT *Detail of the writing on an inscribed lead 'curse' by Honoratus, from the sanctuary of Mercury at Uley, Gloucestershire.*

64 RIGHT *Childbirth amulet from Cholsey, Oxfordshire. This gold foil sheet, incised with a magical text to ensure safe childbirth for a woman named Fabia, would originally have been rolled and worn in a cylindrical case; 2nd or 3rd century AD.*

VI

FARMERS, CRAFTSMEN AND TRADERS

'...bruised beans, two *modii*, chickens, twenty, a hundred apples, if you can find nice ones, a hundred or two hundred eggs, if they are for sale at a fair price... 8 *sextarii* of fish sauce... a *modius* of olives...'

Vindolanda Tablet, shopping list, *c.* AD 100

THIS SHOPPING LIST, written in about AD 100 (see p. 83), concerns supplies to the commander's residence at Vindolanda. Along with that universal desire to procure good quality food at a fair price, the text gives us a snapshot of diet during the Roman period, characterized by two key themes: local seasonal produce, such as apples, and imported foodstuffs, in this case olives and fish sauce, perhaps the comforting tastes of home.

Many types of food and drink consumed in Britain today are a legacy of this period of history, when major changes occurred in the varieties of food that were cultivated, prepared and consumed. Linked to the changes in farming were new and more effective ways of exploiting mineral resources on a scale that had not been seen before in Britain, and arguably would not be seen again until the Industrial Revolution. The large-scale smelting of lead in Britain at this time has even been linked to lead pollution discovered deep in the ice of Iceland.

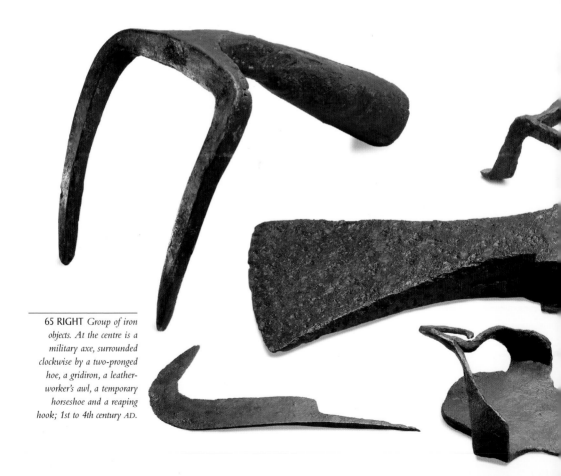

65 RIGHT *Group of iron objects. At the centre is a military axe, surrounded clockwise by a two-pronged hoe, a gridiron, a leatherworker's awl, a temporary horseshoe and a reaping hook; 1st to 4th century AD.*

Much of the British landscape was managed and exploited by the Romans, and the majority of the rural population were engaged in food cultivation or craft activities. In fact, controlling land resources was in many ways *the* most important consideration of the Roman administration: areas with abundant mineral reserves were taken into state control and other land sequestered for army use, or for ex-soldiers, in the case of fields surrounding *coloniae* (see chapter VIII); and private landowners were taxed on their produce.

The most basic subsistence crop introduced by the Romans was spelt wheat, which was apparently preferred to the native emmer or einkorn, although archaeological evidence suggests a preference for barley in the north. Cultivating land required the use of a wooden plough pulled by pairs of oxen, providing not only muscle, but also milk, meat, leather, bone and glue (fig. 76). Iron plough-shares cut the furrow into which seed could be cast or dropped, while manure and compost (of human, animal and food waste) were used to increase soil fertility. The harvest was reaped by hand with a curved iron sickle or a reaping hook, while much larger scythes were used for cutting hay. Such tools formed part of an increased range of iron objects available – the end-products of sustained exploitation of iron ores, especially in the Weald in Kent (fig. 65).

After drying, the wheat was threshed, then ground, or milled, into flour using rotary querns consisting of two closely fitting, circular stones, one of which was fixed to the ground. 'Millstone grit', particularly suitable for making querns, was quarried in the Pennines. Milling was usually done by hand and was a time-consuming and back-breaking process. Skeletal evidence from the Roman cemetery at Poundbury in Dorset implies that it may often have been the lot of women. The end-result was gruel, porridge, barley cakes (flour and milk heated on a stove), or bread, usually wholemeal and unleavened – not the most flavoursome fare, but staple food sufficient to sustain the vast majority of the population.

As well as introducing spelt wheat, the Romans broadened the available range of fruit and vegetables, both locally-grown and imported. Beans and peas were cultivated and many foodstuffs still popular today were introduced, including onion, leek, carrot, parsnip, cucumber, radish and cabbage. Many herbs were also Roman introductions, such as parsley, thyme, marjoram, garlic and mint. There is slight evidence for vineyards, but the climate was barely suitable except in the extreme south, so the grape pips occasionally found probably came from dried grapes (raisins). Dried figs were another Roman import.

66 BELOW A Samian ware vase, found at Felixstowe, Suffolk. It was imported from the continent and is decorated with a hunting scene; 1st century AD.

The principal meats consumed in Roman Britain were beef, mutton and pork – for the latter, the Vindolanda Tablets refer variously to bacon, ham, suckling pig, pork scratching (pig skin), fat and lard. It was rare for animals to be raised exclusively for their meat: cattle, for instance, would only have been slaughtered at the end of their working life when they had ceased to produce good milk yields, a common practice in many poor parts of the world today. Wild game, including wood pigeon, venison and boar, was also eaten, and hunted with spears and arrows or by nets and traps. Fish appear to have played a lesser role in the Roman diet, although apparent lack of evidence might rather reflect the poor survival of fish bones in the archaeological record. There is evidence for the consumption of a very wide range of fish, both freshwater, such as eel, salmon and trout, and salt-

67 ABOVE *An artist's impression of a Roman glassblower's workshop (©David Hill).*

water species like herring and plaice, red mullet and sea bream.

The most common spices on many British dining-tables today are salt and pepper. During the Roman period these were equally important but for different reasons. Pepper was a luxury enjoyed only by the wealthy, as it had to be imported from southern India (fig. 119), whilst salt was absolutely essential to all, as it was the principal means of preservation in the days long before refrigeration. In fact, salt was so valuable that our modern world 'salary' is derived from it. Two Roman *salinae* (salt-pits), one at Droitwich in Worcestershire, and another at Middlewich in Cheshire, have produced archaeological evidence for large-scale salt production, including lead pans that were used to evaporate brine over a hearth. But the estuarine mudflats of the East Anglian coast and Fens seem to have been Britain's principal salt-producing region.

Britain was also the source of exports, as well as imports. At Stonea, in the Cambridgeshire Fens, British Museum excavations unearthed the

68 RIGHT *Amber glass flagon from a grave found at Radnage, Buckinghamshire; 1st century* AD.

remains of a substantial building, possibly the headquarters of an imperial estate, with extensive areas of pasture for grazing sheep, some slaughtered as lambs, probably for salting and export. Another export, British oysters – commonly found on archaeological sites – were a popular delicacy in Rome. The *birrus britannicus*, a type of hooded woollen cloak, is listed in Diocletian's 'Edict of Prices' (AD 301), so was known in other parts of the empire. Beer, a pale yellow ale made from malted barley, might also have been exported, and was certainly consumed, as it, too, is listed in the Vindolanda Tablets. Wine continued to be imported, as it had been from before the conquest (see p. 23).

Large-scale production did not just apply to food, but also to minerals. Clay for making pottery was exploited on a massive scale, much more so than in the preceding Iron Age, and fragments of broken Roman pot still litter many a ploughed field in Britain. New techniques, such as the use of the potter's wheel and slipping, which gave pottery a shiny smooth surface, came to the fore (fig. 16). Industries rose and fell depending on the popularity of their products, which ranged from coarse-wares for the storage, preparation and cooking of food, to fine-wares for use at the table. Pottery was also imported (fig. 66). Imports were often copied: the *mortarium*, for instance, was a new type of Roman 'food mixer', with a rough-gritted interior used for blending herbs and sauces; once imported by the army, *mortaria* were quickly imitated by local potteries (fig. 44).

Related to the pottery industry was glass production, the most basic of which was typically bluish-green, although clear and multi-coloured glass was also made (figs. 68–9). There is no evidence that glass in its raw state was manufactured in

69 BELOW *A blue glass bowl with white marbling, from a grave found at Radnage, Buckinghamshire; 1st century AD.*

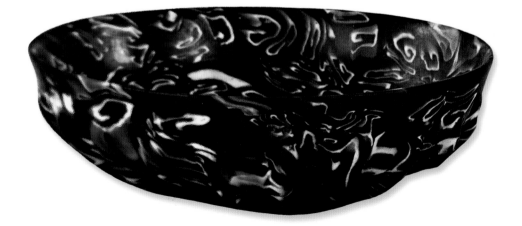

70 ABOVE *Lead canister, decorated with Sol in his chariot, found in a cemetery at Warwick Square, London. Inside the canister, a glass jar (right) contained cremated bone; 2nd to 3rd century AD.*

71 OPPOSITE *Stylized stone head of a woman, from Towcester, Northamptonshire. It was probably part of a monumental tomb set up on nearby Watling Street; 2nd to 3rd century AD.*

Britain, but plenty of evidence that glass vessels were made by skilled glass-blowers using imported blocks or re-used broken glass, technically known as cullet (fig. 67). Glass was popular in Roman Britain for the same qualities we value today: translucent (but not transparent) glass for allowing light through windows; glass bottles and phials for storing liquids such as wine and perfumes; drinking vessels, usually beakers, which became particularly popular in the late Roman period, especially as glass does not taint its contents (fig. 124). The glass bottles used for storing food and liquid were often re-used as containers for cremation burials (fig. 70). Although glass was not produced on the same scale as pottery, many glass-working sites are known, including twenty-one in Roman London, which has also produced the largest dump of cullet − 70 kilograms of production waste found recently near Basinghall Street.

The exploitation of gold and lead has already been discussed (see p. 58). A by-product of lead-working was silver, which was fed into imperial stockpiles, as evidenced by a number of officially stamped ingots

(fig. 115). As for stone, there is virtually no evidence of stone-working before the Roman conquest, so we can imagine that, initially, many masons were immigrants. Most stone-work was probably low-grade, such as roughing and facing, but some would have involved producing dedicatory altars and funerary inscriptions, for which there was considerable demand. The work often shows influences of both native and Roman traditions (fig. 71). Public buildings were built of local stone, for instance London's forum, made of Kentish ragstone. Other quarries are known throughout Britain, as at Barcombe Down near Vindolanda, testament to the major requirements of building projects, such as Hadrian's Wall (see pp. 40–3).

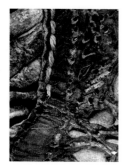

72 BELOW Detail of finely preserved stitching on a pair of leather shoes, found in a sarcophagus at Southfleet, Kent; 3rd to 4th century AD (see also fig. 73 below).

Craftsmen, such as leather-workers, blacksmiths, tanners and carpenters, would frequently be based in towns, usually living at the rear of, or above, their premises (figs. 72–4). No doubt they exchanged their products for food and other items with neighbours and trusted locals, or sold them for hard currency to strangers. Other craftsmen were itinerant, moving between town and country to sell their wares. At temples, metalworkers

73 BELOW A pair of leather shoes made of dark blue leather with gold stitching. They probably belonged to a wealthy woman (see also detail above).

74 RIGHT AND BELOW
*A soldier's shoe (right) and a
hob-nailed shoe (below),
probably for a child;
3rd to 4th century AD.*

produced dedicatory inscriptions on demand, depending on the wishes and resources of the client (fig. 104). One of the most extraordinary survivals of an itinerant worker, or possibly a pair or trio of craftsmen, was discovered at Snettisham in Norfolk in the 1980s (fig. 75). A pottery jar was consigned to the earth some time after AD 155. Its contents are quite extraordinary, as they comprise the craftsmen's complete stock-in-trade: raw material, such as silver bars, imported carnelian, cut and uncut, finished and unfinished finger rings, and the profits of the enterprise in the form of bronze coin. The Snettisham jeweller's hoard is just one example of the wide range and high level of craftsmanship in Roman Britain, the results of which we continue to admire today.

75 Hoard from Snettisham, Norfolk, discovered by a workman in 1985. The hoard consists of the stock-in-trade of one or more jewellery makers from the 2nd century AD.

SILVER INGOTS, *ready for melting and casting into bracelets and rings.*

GEM-SET RINGS, *with intaglios, used to make an impression in wax for sealing documents.*

SILVER SNAKE RINGS *in the form of opposing snake heads (compare the snake bracelets opposite).*

GEMSTONES, *made of carnelian imported from southern India; many are cut with the figures of Classical gods.*

POTTERY JAR, *originally used to store the stash of jewels, coins, and precious stones and metals shown here – probably the abandoned wares of one or more jewellery makers.*

SILVER SNAKE BRACELETS, *decorated with snake heads and snake skin. The snake was popular in Roman times, as it symbolized re-birth and healing (see also the snake rings opposite).*

SCRAP GOLD, *ready to be melted down and made into items of jewellery.*

SILVER AND BRONZE COINS, *struck by a range of Roman emperors, from Nero (AD 54–68) to Antoninus Pius (AD 138–61).*

BURNISHING TOOL, *made of quartz and used to polish the jewellery after casting.*

VII

TOWN AND COUNTRY LIVING

'…think of the high, strident call of the depilator [in the public baths]… never quiet except when he plucks somebody's armpits and makes his customers cry out for him; or the assorted cries of the pastrycook, the sausage seller, the confectioner and all the hawkers of refreshment selling their wares…'

Seneca, *Letters*, LVI, 2, mid-1st century AD

LEFT *Detail of an oil flask, from Aldborough, Yorkshire, depicting a sleeping slave boy awaiting his master; 2nd century AD. (see also fig. 81).*

THE ROMAN EMPIRE'S principal purpose was to exploit the resources of each province for the benefit of its citizens, both locally and in the Mediterranean heartlands. This was achieved through a complex of forts and towns, new types of rural dwellings and systems of land and water management, and a network of connecting roads. Many parts of the British landscape changed dramatically as a result, although this varied greatly across the country. In some remote places, the only evidence of contact with Rome − beyond perhaps the rebuilding of some structures in stone − might be little more than a few sherds of Roman pottery. In other places there is considerable evidence for intensive and long-term occupation.

How individuals were affected was dependent on where they lived, how much they moved around and their place in the social order. An itinerant metalworker, such as the Snettisham jeweller (fig. 75), might have found his life transformed by Rome's influence, allowing him to ply his trade in towns and rural settlements both old and new. On the other hand, a farmer in the north might have been made homeless − probably brutally − when the army deemed his land ideal for the establishment of a new fort, whilst his neighbour only a few miles away was left alone, bar a yearly tax demand of a few *modii* of wheat. The stories of individual lives and experiences are almost completely lost to us, but the transformation of material culture in both town and country gives us glimpses of how secular, cultural and religious life changed under the influence of Rome. The development of

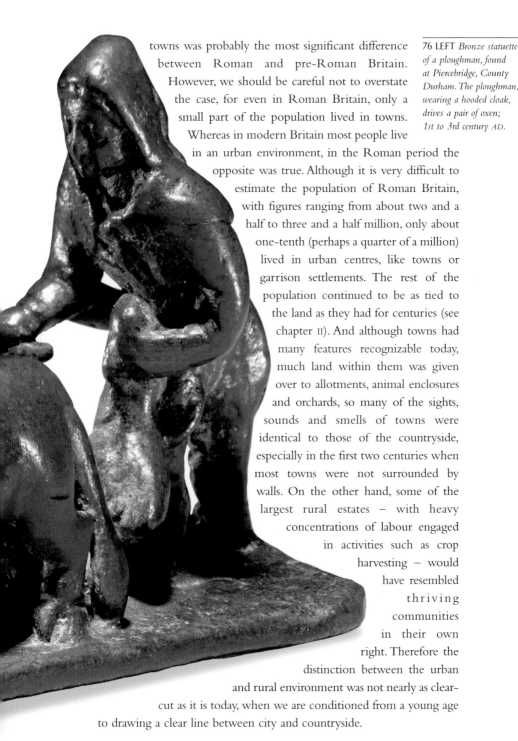

towns was probably the most significant difference between Roman and pre-Roman Britain. However, we should be careful not to overstate the case, for even in Roman Britain, only a small part of the population lived in towns. Whereas in modern Britain most people live in an urban environment, in the Roman period the opposite was true. Although it is very difficult to estimate the population of Roman Britain, with figures ranging from about two and a half to three and a half million, only about one-tenth (perhaps a quarter of a million) lived in urban centres, like towns or garrison settlements. The rest of the population continued to be as tied to the land as they had for centuries (see chapter II). And although towns had many features recognizable today, much land within them was given over to allotments, animal enclosures and orchards, so many of the sights, sounds and smells of towns were identical to those of the countryside, especially in the first two centuries when most towns were not surrounded by walls. On the other hand, some of the largest rural estates – with heavy concentrations of labour engaged in activities such as crop harvesting – would have resembled thriving communities in their own right. Therefore the distinction between the urban and rural environment was not nearly as clear-cut as it is today, when we are conditioned from a young age to drawing a clear line between city and countryside.

76 LEFT *Bronze statuette of a ploughman, found at Piercebridge, County Durham. The ploughman, wearing a hooded cloak, drives a pair of oxen; 1st to 3rd century AD.*

77 An artist's impression of Roman London (*Londinium*) in the 3rd century AD, showing the north bank of the River Thames in the foreground, with the river and Southwark in the background (©Peter Frost/Museum of London).

BACCHUS, *the Roman god of wine, from a mosaic found in 1803 beneath East India House in Leadenhall Street, north of the forum and basilica (town hall).*

FORUM AND BASILICA, *the focus of town life in Roman Britain. The huge basilica, measuring c.150 metres long, was the largest of its kind north of the Alps.*

TOWN WALL, *constructed in the late 2nd century AD, it was made of stone and stood at a height of around 6 metres.*

CRIPPLEGATE FORT, *built in about AD120, probably to house the provincial governor's bodyguard.*

BRONZE HEAD *of the emperor Hadrian (*AD *117–38), discovered in the Thames in 1834.*

TIMBER BRIDGE, *which connected the main part of the town (left) to the smaller settlement in Southwark (right).*

THE WATERFRONT, *where ships from all over the Roman Empire unloaded their cargoes.*

AMPHITHEATRE, *still visible beneath the Guildhall, off Gresham Street. Originally, it had seats for up to 10,000 spectators.*

BRONZE ARCHER *found in Cheapside in 1842, probably representing the hero Hercules.*

ALDERSGATE, *one of six gateways that gave access to the town.*

For the Roman state, towns were nevertheless the essence of 'civilization', with Rome itself providing the ideal model. Towns were a means of organizing and controlling her citizens and subject populations – 'to familiarize the provincials with law-abiding government', as Tacitus puts it, when writing about the town of Colchester (*Annals*, XII, 32, early second century AD). The inauguration of a new town was invested with much symbolism and ceremony, traditionally with the ploughing of a furrow marking its perimeter (fig. 76). The highest status town was the *colonia*, or colony, which was populated by full Roman citizens. In Britain there were four colonies: Colchester, the earliest, established in about AD 49; Lincoln and Gloucester (inaugurated in about AD 90 and AD 96–8 respectively); and York, which was elevated to the status of *colonia* in the early third century (fig. 5). These towns provided retired soldiers and their dependants with a place to settle, and – some have argued – of doing exactly what Tacitus suggests, namely demonstrating to indigenous people what a Roman 'lifestyle' was about. Rome had been establishing such colonies for hundreds of years before the conquest of Britain, and was herself following precedents set by the Greeks and Phoenicians, who had established colonies in distant lands to deal with over-population in the homeland, exploit new resources, and smooth the passage of trade.

Of lesser official status were the *municipia*, self-governing towns in which the inhabitants had rights of citizenship. In Britain only one *municipium* is known for certain, at St. Albans in Hertfordshire. The last two categories were the *civitas* and the *vicus*. The former was very important in Britain, though difficult to define: it was a town of non-Roman citizens granted a certain degree of self-governance. The *civitates* were usually based on old tribal centres, such as *Venta Icenorum* (Caistor-by-Norwich), which was the tribal capital of the Iceni. *Vici* was the name given to small settlements, some of which grew up organically around forts and were populated by those largely dependent on the garrison for their livelihood – Vindolanda provides an excellent example of a *vicus* (see fig. 55).

The archaeological evidence from London provides a sample of town life in Roman Britain (fig. 77). Although its 'official' status is not known, we can be sure that *Londinium* was a Roman foundation, and it rapidly rose to prominence. In modern terms, its area was tiny, but this should not diminish its importance. Roman London lies underneath the modern

79 BELOW *A floor tile, probably from London, which shows a scratched depiction of what appears to be a Roman lighthouse; 1st to 4th century AD.*

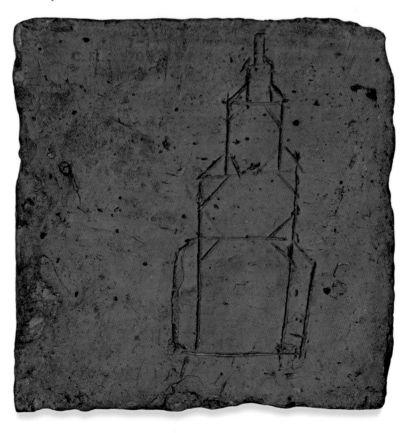

80 LEFT *Bronze head of the emperor Hadrian (AD 117–38), found in the Thames. It is part of a monumental statue, which probably stood in London's forum (see also fig. 77).*

City of London, from the Tower of London in the east to Blackfriars Station in the west, north from Bishopsgate and Cripplegate to Southwark on the Thames' south-bank. Today this area is the heart of London's international financial sector, which is particularly apposite given that Tacitus described Roman London as 'a busy centre, chiefly through its crowd of merchants and stores' (*Annals*, XIV, 33). Even the Bank of England stands on the site of a Roman building: in 1805, when the bank was being extended, part of a mosaic floor was found. At its height in the third century AD, the population of *Londinium* may have reached 30,000.

London quickly became established as the most important mercantile centre of Britannia, with goods arriving from all over the empire and even further afield: pepper and carnelian from India were unloaded at the Thames waterfront, along with amber from the Baltic, perhaps even silk from China.

London was also the seat of government, quickly supplanting Colchester as the base of the provincial governor and the *procurator*, who was responsible for taxes and finance (fig. 78). We know from one of the Vindolanda Tablets that a detachment of Tungrians was sent to support the governor in about AD 95; and a fort was constructed at Cripplegate in the second century AD, probably to house the governor's bodyguard. We also have evidence for the presence of the navy, who, although based principally at Dover in Kent, may have had a London detachment (fig. 79).

81 BELOW *Bronze oil flask, in the form of a young dozing slave who is probably waiting for his master to emerge from the baths; 2nd century AD.*

What were the principal structures of a town like London? At its heart lay the forum, or town square, which provided the focus of administrative, commercial, social and sometimes religious life. It was the place for catching up with friends and family, negotiating business transactions and hearing decrees from the town council. London's forum, at 5,500 square metres, was more modest than St. Albans', a massive expanse of 18,500 square metres; but London's basilica on the northern side of the forum was the largest in north-west Europe: its scale, *c.*150 metres long, must reflect its importance as the likely base for the offices of the governor and *procurator* and their considerable entourage of civil servants. The basilica was also where the town council met to agree business, where court cases were tried, and legal disputes heard. Running along the forum's remaining sides were shops, temporary stalls and other administrative offices. The forum was also the place where Rome could remind the population of its power by the erection of imposing statues, sculptures and inscriptions (fig. 80).

82 RIGHT *A collection of hairpins in silver and bone, from London; 1st to 3rd centuries* AD.

Many towns had public baths, and London had at least three, the largest at Huggin Hill on Upper Thames Street (fig. 81). In addition to cleansing, baths functioned as places in which to socialize, exercise and even, on occasion, to have a shave, a haircut, or receive cosmetic or medical treatment (fig. 82). The baths also attracted snack vendors: at the Caerleon baths, deposits of chicken and sheep bone imply snacks of drumsticks and chops. Such evidence chimes with Seneca's complaint that public baths were noisy, rowdy places, the peace disturbed with the cries of 'pastry cooks, sausage sellers and confectioners' (*Letters*, 56, mid first century AD).

Centres of equal rowdiness – the amphitheatre and the circus – were two other Roman 'imports'. About twenty British amphitheatres have been located in town and country, some (like Silchester, Caerleon and Chester), well-preserved and extensively excavated; others only suggested by a few surviving traces of their elliptical earth embankments. London's amphitheatre was discovered in 1988 beneath the medieval Guildhall; it was built in about AD 70, shortly before Rome's Colosseum, and in use until about AD 300. It could hold somewhere between 7,000 and 10,000 spectators. Amphitheatres were venues often associated with combat and the spilling of blood, pitting men against wild animals, mainly locally caught, and providing the setting for public executions; but some arenas might also have doubled up as theatres and for milder entertainments such as acrobatics. Professional gladiators may have

83 ABOVE *A bronze gladiator's helmet, from Hawkedon, Suffolk. It may have belonged to a gladiator based at nearby Colchester during the 1st century AD.*

appeared sometimes, and troupes are known to have travelled the empire, but there is only limited evidence for gladiators in Britain (figs. 83–4). It was not until 2004 that the remains of a circus (a chariot-racing track) were identified in Britain. Discovered at Colchester, rather appropriately beneath modern garrison buildings about half a kilometre south of the town, the circus had eight starting-gates and a track length of just over 400 metres. Races would probably have involved chariots of two or four horses, and it has been estimated that there was capacity for 8,000 spectators (fig. 85).

The cosmopolitan nature of religious life in London is clear from archaeological discoveries. A range of different gods, cults and, what to modern sensibilities might be considered unsavoury religious practices, can be documented. Bacchus is depicted on a mosaic from Leadenhall Street in the City, found during building works on the offices of the East India Company in 1803 (fig. 86). The mosaic's reference to Bacchus' mythical visit to India, provides a fitting connection with the placing of the East India Company offices in the same location centuries later! Evidence for the worship of Hercules comes from a number of bronze statuettes and figurines, the most sophisticated of which shows the hero as an archer (fig. 87). Hercules' popularity is easily understood, particular amongst male devotees, as he was the epitome of strength, courage and masculinity. Eastern 'mystery' cults were also popular and well-attested in London. The most famous is the cult of Mithras, a sun god of Indo-

84 ABOVE AND LEFT
Bone figurine of a gladiator
of the murmillo *class, from*
Colchester, Essex. His shield
(above) shows him defeating
his opponent, a lightly armed
retiarius (a gladiator, who
carried a trident and net);
1st to 3rd century AD.

85 LEFT *Glass beaker, from
Colchester, Essex, depicting a
chariot race. The inscription
around the rim records the
victory of Cresces, one of the
charioteers; 1st century* AD.

86 ABOVE *Mosaic found in
Leadenhall Street, London,
showing Bacchus riding a
tiger; 1st to 2nd century* AD.

Iranian origin. The discovery of substantial remains of a mithraeum near Mansion House caused quite a stir in the 1950's. Bull sacrifice was also an element of the cult of Mithras and that of Cybele, the Great Mother Goddess, and an ornate bronze clamp found in the Thames may have been used to castrate her priests (fig. 88). Egyptian gods, such as Harpocrates, were also worshipped (fig. 89). All towns had cemeteries, and Roman law required that these were placed outside the inhabited area, usually flanking roads leading out of town. The tomb of the *procurator* Classicianus (fig. 26), for instance, was probably located in a cemetery to the east of London near Aldgate High Street, which was still in use at least 250 years later (fig. 90).

With a few exceptions such as the *coloniae,* most towns did not have walls until the second century AD. As a general rule earth and timber structures were gradually replaced with stone. The London wall, constructed in about AD 200, was fairly typical: it was built of Kentish ragstone to a thickness of roughly 2 metres and a height of about 6 metres, with a ditch in front and a bank behind. In the fourth century AD, the wall was extended along the river frontage and bastion towers were added, in common with other towns in the province (fig. 77). Although town walls were important for protection, they were equally symbols of progress, civic pride and community, and also made the distinction between town and countryside clear.

87 RIGHT *Bronze statuette of an archer, from Cheapside, London. It probably represents the hero Hercules shooting the Birds of Stymphalos, one of his twelve labours; 2nd century AD.*

Despite the growth of towns, the majority of the population of Britain remained rurally based. The range of different types of settlement was extensive, and our understanding of it has been transformed in recent decades by aerial survey and the recording of scatters of archaeological finds. In addition to the larger 'official' towns, like Lincoln, St. Albans and Silchester, and military garrisons (see chapters III and IV); other concentrated settlements, like Baldock in Hertfordshire, have been termed 'small towns', as they have only some of the features of the larger urban centres. At the lower end of the scale, individual farmsteads might house just a few occupants living in one central, simple single-roomed dwelling that served as the centre for much daily life. These dwellings were constructed of timber with clay-daub or drystone walling. They could be rectangular but were usually circular or ovoid, which dispels the myth that the 'roundhouse' disappeared with the advent of Rome.

The most distinctive new type of Roman rural dwelling was the villa. Although villas vary hugely, characteristically they are rectangular

buildings of stone, mortared brick or half-timber construction, with tiled or thatched roofs and clusters of rooms, sometimes as many as seventy. Some had private bath suites, painted wall plaster, floor mosaics and under-floor heating – the latter feature was a specific adaptation to the British climate. The main 'villa zone' covers central and southern England, East Anglia, Lincolnshire, the east Midlands, the Cotswolds and Somerset; and the largest and wealthiest villas mostly date from the mid-second to the fourth century AD.

88 BELOW *Bronze castration clamp from the River Thames, possibly used during the castration rituals for priests of Cybele; 2nd to 3rd century AD.*

In the past, villas were seen in rather simplistic terms as country retreats for the landed gentry. Some conform to that perception – it has been suggested, for example, that Fishbourne in Sussex was a residence of the provincial governor. But now that archaeologists focus not just on the main house, but also on ancillary buildings, which could be very substantial, it is becoming apparent that the picture was more complex (fig. 91). One of the most intensely excavated villas is Lullingstone in Kent (figs. 5 and 92). Lullingstone was built in the second century AD, with a

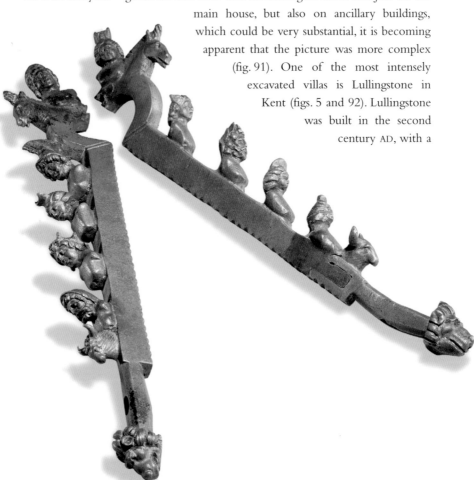

89 LEFT *Silver statuette of the Egyptian deity Harpocrates (Horus), found in the River Thames, London; 1st to 2nd century AD.*

90 ABOVE *Ragstone sarcophagus from the Minories, East London. Inside was the skeleton of a boy of about twelve years old, whose portrait appears on the outside of the coffin; late 3rd to 4th century AD.*

corridor at the back and a veranda at the front linking wings on either side of a central block of rooms; there might also have been an upper floor. Evidence suggests it was a working farm, with the surrounding fields used to grow wheat, vegetables and possibly fruit trees, to raise livestock and perhaps to keep bees. Some outbuildings were used to store the products of the harvest, and the river Darent may have provided a convenient means of transport north to the Thames estuary and the markets of London. In about AD 150, the owners added a suite of baths, initially supplied by a well, but later by a small aqueduct channelling water from higher up the valley. The expansion of Lullingstone implies that the owners produced enough surplus to invest in and embellish their property.

But the story is not quite that simple. Lullingstone has religious elements, which suggest that it was not just a farm estate or a country retreat. In one corner a 'cult room' had been constructed with a deep cellar; around the cult room, fragments of wall paintings depict water nymphs, implying that the room was a shrine to a river deity, perhaps the 'nymph' of the river Darent. But also found in the cult room were two marble busts; it has been suggested that one depicts the Roman emperor Pertinax, governor of Britain between AD 185 and 187, before he became one of the shortest-lived emperors in Rome's history – his reign during AD 193 lasting only eighty-six days (fig. 93). So was the cult room dedicated to the 'imperial cult', too, or had the villa even been at some stage Pertinax's private residence? Furthermore, at the end of its occupation in the fourth century, Lullingstone also provides evidence for Christianity: a small house church was constructed over the cult room, represented by surviving fragments of wall paintings depicting Christian Chi-Rho motifs (combining the first two letters of Christ's name in Greek), and praying Christian figures (fig. 94). In addition, a new floor mosaic, which had been laid in the grandest room of the house, includes a depiction of Bellerophon slaying the Chimera, thought to be a representation of good triumphing over evil (see p. 141).

The evidence suggests Lullingstone was the residence of a wealthy estate owner, but it might also have become a place of pilgrimage for those who wished to honour the water nymph, or for an imperial cult, and later for Christ. Such a complex sequence of useage may well have occurred more widely, for religion appears to have permeated all aspects of life in Roman Britain.

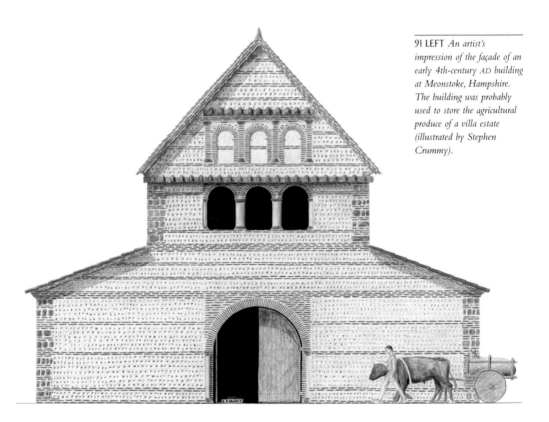

91 LEFT *An artist's impression of the façade of an early 4th-century AD building at Meonstoke, Hampshire. The building was probably used to store the agricultural produce of a villa estate (illustrated by Stephen Crummy).*

92 ABOVE *An artist's impression of the villa estate at Lullingstone, Kent, as it might have appeared in the late 4th century AD (© Peter Urmston/English Heritage Photo Library).*

93 RIGHT *Marble bust, one of two portrait heads found at Lullingstone, Kent. It is thought that it may depict the emperor Pertinax (AD 193).*

94 LEFT *Wall painting from Lullingstone, Kent, depicting a group of praying Christians; 4th century AD.*

VIII

HEALTH, MAGIC AND GODS

'To unconquerable Silvanus, Gaius Tetius Veturius Micianus, prefect of the Sebosian Cavalry Regiment, on fulfilment of his vow willingly set up this [altar] for taking a wild boar of such remarkable fineness which many of his predecessors had been unable to bag.'

Roman Inscriptions of Britain, 1041

LEFT *Detail of a horse-and-rider figurine, found in Cambridgeshire; 3rd to 4th century* AD *(see also fig. 99).*

95 **RIGHT** *Bronze figurine of Aesculapius from near Chichester, West Sussex – the only representation of the god found in Britain to date; 1st to 4th century* AD.

So RUNS AN INSCRIPTION on an altar, found near Stanhope in County Durham, dedicated by a cavalry officer to the god Silvanus, a spirit of the woods (see p. 121). We know nothing else about the life of Micianus, but his act of devotion tells us much about the attitude of people to religion during the Roman period.

Before embarking on the boar hunt, Micianus said a prayer, asking the appropriate god for divine assistance in bagging the prize boar. Having successfully hunted and killed the animal, he naturally put his success down to divine favour and not his skills as a huntsman. As Silvanus had kept his side of the bargain, Micianus then went to considerable effort, and probably no little expense, to have an altar inscribed in honour of the god, commemorating the event. No doubt he and others then used the altar to make sacrificial offerings to Silvanus, maybe an animal, or sometimes more simple fare like fruit and cakes, in order to keep the god on-side and ensure success in future hunting expeditions.

Micianus was not alone. We can be certain that virtually the whole population of Roman Britain, from the provincial governor down to the lowliest labourer believed that there were many gods inhabiting the earth, air, sky and water, in this world and the next, who influenced every aspect of life and death.

Relationships

96 LEFT *Clay statuette of a mother-goddess found at Welwyn, Hertfordshire, but made in Gaul. She is seated in a wicker chair suckling an infant; 2nd century AD.*

with the gods were contractual, and by the process of honouring a god – whether by tossing a coin into a spring, investing in a new cult statue, or, for the very rich, paying for the construction of a new temple – people believed that they could engage the gods to order the cosmos and influence the world in their favour.

How did such a situation arise in which superstition seems to be all pervading? There are two principal reasons. Firstly, much of the natural world was mysterious and often terrifying, and natural processes, largely misunderstood, were associated with the will of the gods. For example, in the Roman world, a bolt of lightning striking a tree, or worse a person, would have been viewed as the divine judgement of Jupiter. (The Celts believed something very similar: emissaries to the court of Alexander the Great in 335 BC said that the greatest thing they feared was the sky falling on their heads.) Secondly, life was very unpredictable and easily lost: a particularly heavy frost might ravage crops, and lead to famine; fire might rapidly destroy half a town; a flash flood could sweep away a farmer's livestock and, with it, his livelihood. At a personal level, many women died in childbirth, and infant mortality was very high. The honouring of mother goddesses and female protectors (for instance Minerva) was a natural response (fig. 96). Similar concerns are reflected today in the numerous shrines in Catholic and Orthodox Christian countries dedicated to the Virgin Mary, the mother of Christ. Furthermore, health was fragile: ailments like diarrhoea and influenza could be deadly; cuts and grazes could turn septic; and even apparently minor battle wounds might prove fatal. Quite simply, it was critical not to become ill, for the difficulty in curing the sick was all too apparent. Environment, diet, exercise, hygiene

97 ABOVE *Lindow Man, a well-preserved body found on the edge of Lindow Moss, Cheshire. He died in about AD 60.*

98 BELOW *A selection of bronze figurines from Southbroom, Wiltshire, depicting a number of different Roman deities; 3rd century* AD.

and doctors all had a part to play, but so too did the gods, who were believed – by patient and doctor alike – to control disease. Some had particular links to health, such as Minerva and Apollo and their native counterparts, but the greatest Roman healer god was Aesculapius, famous for his miracle cures often involving sacred snakes (fig. 95).

The Roman state was generally tolerant of other religions, and in any case found that many of its own beliefs were shared. One exception from the viewpoint of the indigenous Britons may have been the 'Cult of the Deified Emperors'. This was the belief promoted by the Roman state that upon death emperors became gods, and temples were constructed in their honour. Antagonism towards this concept was not necessarily ideological, for the burial sites of British tribal chiefs were probably also places of pilgrimage, but because the imperial cult was a powerful symbol of the Roman occupation. Thus the temple to Claudius at Colchester, constructed soon after the conquest, was a target during the Boudican revolt (see pp. 36–7 and fig. 24). It is possible that the head of Hadrian

(fig. 80), which probably stood in London's forum, was hacked off the statue and thrown into the Thames as an act of iconoclasm (the destruction of objects of veneration). Equally, some aspects of native British religion were abhorrent to the Romans, particularly human sacrifice, which may have been practised by the Druids, although we should be cautious, for most of what we know about the Druids comes from biased Roman writers. It may be that Lindow Man, one of a number of European 'bog bodies' (fig. 97), was one such sacrifice: radiocarbon dating indicated that he was killed in about AD 60, perhaps not coincidentally, just at the time when the Roman governor Paullinus was making his way through Cheshire to destroy the last Druid stronghold on Anglesey. Generally, however, the Romans sought accommodation with native cults through a process termed 'syncretism', whereby two similar deities were conflated. Examples include a set of figurines from Southbroom in Wiltshire, which portray Roman gods like Mercury in a distinctive 'native' style (fig. 98). Another example comes from Felmingham in Norfolk (fig. 100), where the head of Jupiter, chief

99 RIGHT *A bronze figurine of a horse-and rider-god from Stow-cum-Quy, Cambridgeshire; 3rd to 4th century AD (see also p. 120).*

Roman sky god, was found together with symbols of local belief, such as a wheel likely to represent Taranis, the Celtic god of change.

How were religious beliefs practised and gods honoured? At a personal level, people often wore items designed to protect themselves against evil spirits and demonstrate their personal beliefs to others. Roman snake rings, a good example of this custom, were a new type of jewellery in Britain, appearing in large numbers during the first to second centuries AD. The snake, because of its ability to shed its skin, was associated with renewal and healing and especially with the god Aesculapius; it was only after Christianity took root (see pp. 133–41) that the snake became associated with temptation and evil. Finger rings with the letters 'ToT' probably refer to 'Toutatis', a sky god conflated with Jupiter or, in one instance, with Mars (fig. 101). Other people carried small cult images around with them. A merchant might choose a figure of Mercury, a god who watched over travellers, while a soldier might prefer a representation of the war god Mars or the hero Hercules (fig. 87). There were also more specialized local cults, many of which were unique to Britain. A 'horse-and-rider' cult has been identified, and although we do not know the name of the local god being honoured, he clearly had affinities with Mars. The evidence for this cult comes in the form of small statuettes and enamelled plate brooches (see pp. 120–1 and fig. 99). As well as items carried on the person, many houses and public buildings would have had a small shrine (*lararium*) where images of gods were placed. Honouring these deities was a way of trying to protect the home from natural catastrophes or the unwelcome attentions of enemies or thieves.

Just like modern-day churches, mosques and synagogues, large numbers of temples and religious sanctuaries existed in Britain during the Roman period. These were either entirely new structures or ones based on pre-existing cult sites, which were expanded and consolidated after the Roman conquest. Most had a central sacred building in which the cult statue was placed, access to which was restricted to priests (fig. 103), and an outer perimeter area for private devotees. Offerings using dedicated stone altars, like that set up to Silvanus by Micianus (see pp. 121–2), were made outside the temple, and often involved animal sacrifice and the pouring of libations (fig. 102), a process designed to symbolically nourish the deity in question, and so ensure their continued favour. Offerings and thanks might also take more solid material forms, such as gold, silver

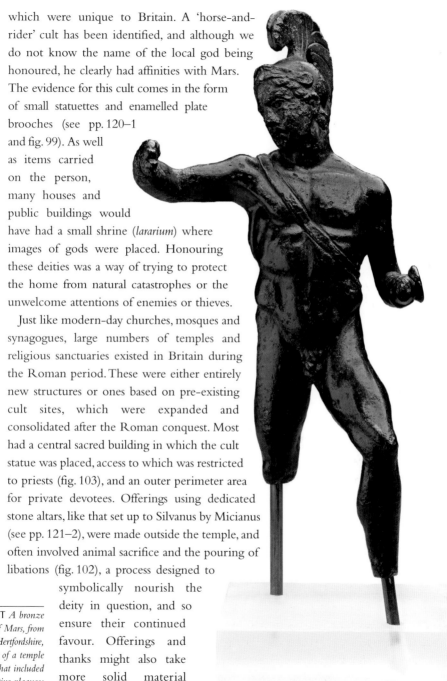

101 RIGHT *A bronze figurine of Mars, from Barkway, Hertfordshire, part of a temple deposit that included large silver votive plaques; 2nd to 3rd century* AD.

or bronze votive plaques inscribed with dedications and pinned up around a cult statue (fig. 104). Another related activity was the placing of lead curse tablets at sanctuary sites like Uley in Gloucester (fig. 62–3). One devotee curses 'him who has stolen my hooded cloak', and asks the god (in this case, Mercury) to inflict death, insomnia and impotency on the thief, although the inscriber adds the caveat that, if the wrong is righted, the curse should be lifted (see also pp. 78–80).

In some places, temple complexes were closely associated with places of physical well-being and natural beauty. There are a number of sites in Britain centred around spring heads; above all the thermal springs at Bath which has some of Britain's best preserved Roman remains (figs. 105–6).

102 ABOVE *A bronze pan from a grave at Faversham, Kent. In the centre is a relief of the head of Medusa with inlaid silver eyes, whilst the head of Pan appears on the handle; 1st century* AD.

Every day, a quarter of a million gallons of hot, iron-rich water still gush out of the earth at Bath, and the perceived health benefits of the waters were as popular in Roman Britain as in more recent times. A bath complex in association with temples grew up around the springs, which fed a series of different therapeutic pools, and vast numbers of offerings were made by people seeking physical and spiritual well-being from Sulis, the native deity of the spring, who was conflated with Roman Minerva. Similar religious sites around springs developed at Springhead in Kent, Lydney in Gloucestershire, and Buxton in Derbyshire, still a famous supply of mineral water. A temple treasure recently discovered at Ashwell in Hertfordshire (fig. 104), probably represents a temple dedicated to Senuna, most likely a goddess of a spring, who was also associated with Minerva. Springs were venerated because the role of water as the principal source of life was well understood, and people lived in fear of springs drying up; but water at shrines also came to symbolize the cleansing and renewal of the spirit. Springs were seen as the exact opposite of bogs and marshes, with their black stagnant waters into which the careless traveller could easily meet their end, and which were sometimes used as the burial places for acts of ritual sacrifice (see p. 125). Such treacherous locations may have been regarded as the realm of underground gods, and perhaps even as entrances to the Underworld.

But it was not just Roman and home-grown deities that were popular in Britain. Smaller cults, largely from the eastern Mediterranean, were also introduced during the Roman period, and reflect the multicultural nature of the populace. These deities included Isis, Mithras and Cybele, evidence for all of whom is well known in some places, for instance in London (see p. 112). These cults often focused on the idea of one supreme god and, as time passed, more and more people gravitated towards the idea of a single, overarching deity. All these 'monotheistic' cults died out in time, except for one, the Christian: three centuries after Christ's crucifixion, Constantine's official recognition of Christianity made it the principal religion of the Western world, and in Britain it remains one of the longest-lasting legacies of the Roman period. The province has some of the earliest physical remains of Christian belief in the whole of the Roman Empire, although it is often mixed with belief in the old pagan

105 ABOVE *Gilt-silver vessel handle from Capheaton, Northumberland, showing Minerva standing above a spring and temple. The scene may represent the sacred springs at Bath; 2nd century AD.*

104 LEFT *Selected items from a temple hoard near Ashwell, Hertfordshire, found at a shrine based around a spring; 3rd century AD.*

gods. In the Mildenhall treasure (fig. 121), for example, most of the imagery revolves around the worship of Bacchus, the god of wine (fig. 107), yet hints of Christian belief appear on a few of the spoons, bearing the Chi-Rho symbol (combining the first two letters of Christ's name in Greek). A common Christian formula, the Chi-Rho also appears on finger rings (fig. 110).

One unambiguously Christian find is a hoard from Water Newton in Cambridgeshire (Roman *Durobrivae*) (figs. 5 and 108). Dating to the late fourth century AD, the hoard incorporates the earliest set of Christian vessels from the Roman Empire. The vessels may have been used to decant and drink wine and share communal bread as part of the Christian ritual of the Eucharist, or Holy Communion. The other main Christian ceremony, then

106 ABOVE *The Great Bath at Bath, Somerset, part of a sacred springs complex. It originally had a barrel-vaulted ceiling, 40 metres high; 2nd century* AD *(© RH Productions).*

107 RIGHT *Marble statue of Bacchus found in the villa at Spoonley Wood, Gloucestershire. The god holds a wine cup and at his feet sits his panther; 3rd to 4th century* AD.

108 Hoard of silver, from the Roman town of Water Newton, Cambridgeshire. Probably the possession of a small Christian community, it was buried around the late 4th century AD, and found by a metal-detector user in 1975.

SILVER JUG, *originally with a handle, and decorated with leaf and plant motifs. It was probably used to hold wine during early Christian rituals.*

SILVER BOWL, *inscribed in Latin around the rim with the dedication, 'Innocentia and Viventia present this vessel to Christ'. Christ is represented by the Chi-Rho symbol (see inset below).*

CHI-RHO VOTIVE PLAQUE, *probably pinned around an altar or statue. It is impressed with a gilded Chi-Rho symbol, formed from the first two letters of Christ's name in Greek (Χριστόζ). On the right and left, between the arms of the Chi, appear the first and last letters of the Greek alphabet, alpha (Α) and omega (ω), symbolic of Christ as the 'beginning' and 'end'.*

WATER NEWTON TREASURE 4TH CENTURY AD

HANGING LAMP *(restored),* *made of thin sheet silver. It was originally furnished with a candle, and hung from a ceiling to cast light, possibly inside a Christian chapel.*

SILVER CUP, *one of three bowls or cups in the treasure, which may have been used for drinking wine, as part of an early Christian ritual.*

SILVER DISH, *in the centre of which appears a lightly incised Chi-Rho (see opposite), accompanied by the Greek letters, alpha and omega. The dish may have been used for sharing bread as part of an early Christian ritual.*

SILVER BOWL, *inscribed in Latin with the words, 'O Lord, I Publianus, relying on you, honour your holy altar [or sanctuary]'. The inscription indicates that the treasure probably belonged to a church used by a community of Christian worshippers.*

as now, was baptism, and there are a few examples of what are believed to be lead baptismal fonts, including one from Icklingham (fig. 109). The Water Newton hoard also included a series of triangular silver plaques displaying the Chi-Rho symbol. Some also incorporated a Greek Alpha (α) and omega (ω), the first and last letters of the Greek alphabet – a Biblical reference to Christ representing 'the beginning' and 'the end'. Despite its Christian symbolism, even the Water Newton hoard can be linked to Britain's pagan past, for the silver plaques, which were probably placed on, or pinned around, a Christian altar, are Christian versions of the pagan votive plaques invoking deities like Senuna at Ashwell (see p. 131). A similar practice of pinning votive plaques on or around altars, statues and icons continues in many parts of the Christian orthodox world today.

109 BELOW *Lead tank from Icklingham, Suffolk, bearing a Chi-Rho symbol. The tank was probably used for baptism as part of early Christian ceremonies; 4th century AD.*

There are indications that, until the fourth century AD, Christians were nervous of worshipping Christ openly, probably fearing persecution from non-believers. A pewter platter from Stamford in Lincolnshire, for example, shows hidden in its inscribed decoration what appears to be a Chi-Rho symbol (fig. 111). Although Constantine had established an 'Edict of Toleration' in AD 313, the emperor Julian (AD 360–3) sought to reverse Constantine's policy, and might have actively encouraged the persecution of the Christian minority.

Although some foundations of buildings have been argued to be the sites of churches and Christian chapels, two particular places show strong evidence for the presence of Christian worshippers. One is a probable house-church at Lullingstone in Kent (see pp. 114–17). The other is more

110 ABOVE *Gold finger rings from Brentwood, Essex and Suffolk. They bear the Chi-Rho symbol, so would have been worn by Christians; 4th century AD.*

III LEFT *Pewter vessels from Stamford, Leicestershire and Church Norton, West Sussex. Both vessels were probably used during Christian ceremonies; 4th century AD.*

112 BELOW *The centrepiece of a large floor mosaic, from Hinton St Mary, Dorset, thought to depict the head of Christ; 4th century AD.*

difficult to interpret. In the centre of a large mosaic floor uncovered at Hinton St Mary in Dorset is what appears to be one of the earliest depictions of Christ (fig. 112). The portrait shows a togate figure with a Chi-Rho symbol behind his head, flanked by pomegranates, symbolic of eternal life. In addition, another part of the mosaic shows the pagan hero Bellerophon slaying the mythic Chimera. It was an episode often found in Christian contexts, including at Lullingstone (see pp. 116–17), and was symbolic of the triumph of good over evil. However, debate continues over the interpretation of the head, because the image also bears a resemblance to one or two fourth-century Roman emperors, including Constantine the Great (AD 307–37) and Magnentius (AD 350–3). Whatever the case, the apparent prosperity of southern Britain in the late fourth century was about to undergo radical change, as Britain slipped out of Roman control.

BRITONS AFTER ROME

'...the barbarians from across the Rhine attacked everywhere with all their strength.... the inhabitants of Britain were obliged to throw off Roman rule and lived independently, no longer subject to Roman laws.'

Zosimus, *New History,* VI, 5, 2–3,

c. late 5th century AD

LEFT *Detail of the 'Great Dish' from the Mildenhall treasure; 4th century AD (see also fig. 121).*

113 RIGHT *Silver coin of the rebel emperor Carausius (AD 286–93), with the head of Oceanus, possibly a reference to the Channel.*

UNLIKE THE OFFICIAL END OF WORLD WAR II in Europe on 8 May 1945, it is not possible to pinpoint a single day – or, indeed, a year – when the province of Britannia was no longer 'officially' part of the Roman Empire. The best that can be said is that by approximately AD 410, i.e. around 1,600 years ago, Rome had ceased to administer its most northerly province. In the immediate period that followed, life for many in isolated rural areas probably continued much as normal, but others may have found their world transformed, particularly by the arrival of new migrants. The period of British history that is termed 'Anglo-Saxon' had begun.

114 ABOVE *Gold medallion of Constantius I (AD 293–306), struck at Trier, Germany. It commemorates the defeat of the rebel emperor Allectus. Constantius I is raising Britannia from her knees.*

The contemporary historical evidence for the 'end' of Roman Britain is patchy and mainly of dubious reliability. The late fifth-century writings of the Greek historian Zosimus exemplify this problem. In one place he tells us that the Britons in the early fifth century 'were obliged to throw off Roman rule and live independently, no longer subject to Roman laws'. In another passage, specifically dated to AD 410, he says that the Britons appealed to the emperor Honorius for help and were advised to 'look after their own affairs' (*New History*, VI, 10, 2, *c.* late fifth century AD). But most scholars now believe that this second passage, coming as it does in a section discussing Italy, does not relate to Britannia, but rather to *Brittia*, the Greek spelling for *Bruttium* in southern Italy, and was an error made when the text was later copied. Such unreliable historical evidence means that the period from roughly AD 400 to 550 is often unhelpfully termed 'the Dark Ages', a period to which the legendary King Arthur is traditionally assigned – a myth largely the stuff of medieval romance.

Because of the paucity of the historical sources, our attention is directed instead to archaeology. The material remains can be divided into two categories: evidence for the decline of Roman Britain and evidence for life in the immediate post-Roman period. Evidence for decline is not difficult to find, and shows that, at least politically, Britain was in trouble from about the early third century AD. During this period, the military were required to defend Roman territory

115 ABOVE *Hoard of silver coins, bullion, cut plate and bowl from Coleraine, Northern Ireland; late 4th to early 5th century AD.*

on an increasing number of fronts: in addition to the troop–heavy zone around Hadrian's Wall, which continued to be garrisoned into the late fourth century, new forts began to appear around parts of the British coast, particularly in East Anglia and the south-east. This chain of new and existing installations stretched from Brancaster in Norfolk all the way to Portchester in Hampshire on the south coast (figs. 5 and 122). These defences, known as 'the Saxon Shore', were part of a wider defensive system on the north French coast, which ran from Britanny to Belgium. On the west coast of Britain, too, forts continued to be occupied at places like Cardiff, Caerleon, Caernarvon and Maryport, while the north-east and north-west coasts were equipped with a series of signal stations by the fourth century AD.

The Saxon Shore forts were usually not linked to the existing road network, demonstrating that their role was outward, facing towards the

116 ABOVE *Bronze belt-buckle from Catterick, North Yorkshire, decorated with sea horses and dolphins. It probably belonged to an army officer; late 4th to early 5th century AD.*

117 OPPOSITE *Gold bracelets from the Hoxne treasure, Suffolk, part of the largest hoard of Roman gold and silver found in Britain; late 4th century AD (see also fig. 119).*

sea. So, as the Picts from modern-day Scotland continued to breach Hadrian's Wall, sea-borne raids began in earnest. The Scotti from Ireland launched attacks across the Irish Sea into the west of Britain, arguably the wealthiest part of the province at this time. Rather better known are raids around the Channel coastline, from parts of free Germany, by the Jutes, Saxons and Angles, from which the name England, a corruption of 'Angleland', ultimately derives. In AD 367, there are historical references to a joining of forces in a plot widely termed 'the Barbarian conspiracy'. Specific archaeological evidence for this event may be lacking, but the strengthening of coastal defences at least proves that the threat was real.

What was the purpose of these incursions? Some may have had political motives, such as the settling of old scores, but most were probably economically driven. Hoards of late Roman silver coin and 'hacksilver' (cut-up pieces of Roman plate) found in Scotland and Ireland (fig. 115) may be direct archaeological evidence for the spoils of such raids or, alternatively, evidence of appeasement. Either way, the fact is that large quantities of wealth found their way into the hands of people, whom Rome would have considered 'barbarians'. Another motivation was undoubtedly slavery, although the scale of human trafficking is unknown. The most famous documented instance of kidnap and enslavement is that of Patrick, the patron saint of Ireland, who grew up in the west of Britain, probably from a wealthy 'Romanized' family. At the age of sixteen – probably in the early or mid-fifth century AD – Patrick was kidnapped and forced into serfdom in Ireland, no doubt alongside many others, whose stories will never be known.

Yet it was not just external problems that beset the province in the last few decades of Roman rule. Civil unrest, too, was undoubtedly endemic. Part of the problem derived from the fact that, as a frontier province, Britain was by default top-heavy with military personnel (fig. 116). A succession of military commanders are known to have used Britain's troops to pursue political power – Carausius is probably the most famous example. From his naval base at Gesoriacum (modern Boulogne), he was assigned the task of intercepting Saxon and Frankish raiders but, when accused of collusion with the enemy, fled with his loyal troops to Britain,

118 ABOVE *Silver* lanx *(tray), found at Corbridge, Northumberland in 1735. The vessel depicts the god Apollo in his shrine on the island of Delos, Greece; 4th century AD.*

proclaimed himself emperor and for a while controlled Britain and northern Gaul. In AD 293, Carausius was assassinated by his own finance minister Allectus, who briefly assumed his position (figs. 113–4). Such 'coups' continued throughout the fourth century, culminating in the elevation of Gratian (AD 367–83) to imperial status by the British troops. The round of revolts and attempts to become emperor ended with the failure of Constantine III to seize control of Gaul and Britain – just as Carausius had before him – although he almost certainly extracted the last remaining troops from Britain before his assassination in Gaul in AD 411.

Archaeologically, the collapse in the markers of 'Romanization' are quite dramatic. Even though there is some evidence of the occupation of towns beyond the late fourth century AD (e.g. at Silchester and Canterbury), there was nothing like the scale of

building that was seen in the first three hundred years of Roman rule. Town defences lapsed into disrepair, amphitheatres, forums and public baths fell out of use and their building materials were re-used in later buildings such as churches. The setting up of inscriptions seems to have virtually ceased: tombstones, inaugural and dedicatory inscriptions almost vanish. The large-scale production of pottery and metalwork and the importation of goods, such as wine and olive oil, largely dried up. Particularly striking is the collapse of coinage: even though the Roman emperor Honorius continued to issue coins up until his death in AD 423, no new coin was supplied to Britain after about AD 408. The cessation of coinage supplies meant it was no longer possible for the army and civil administrators to be paid and, without pay, they were no longer obliged to carry out their duties. Some attempt was made to continue coin production, with the edges of silver coins clipped, and the clippings made into new coins, but this relied entirely on the existing circulation pool, so it was not a long-term solution. A system of regular coinage would not be

119 ABOVE *A silver-gilt pepper-pot in the form of a late Roman lady, one of four similar tableware items in the Hoxne treasure, Suffolk; late 4th century AD.*

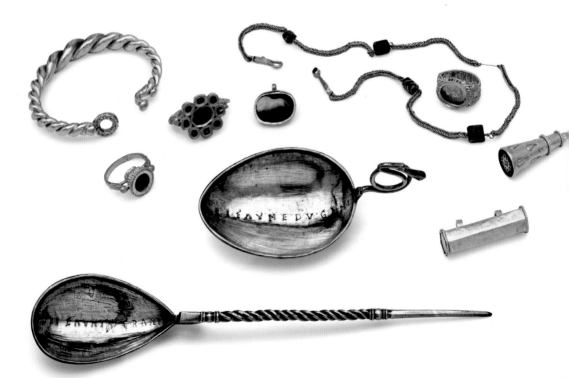

120 ABOVE AND LEFT
The Thetford treasure, found in Norfolk, includes a range of gold jewellery and silver tableware, such as the gold rings, bracelets, pendants and silver spoons (left), dedicated to the god Faunus. The plate of the gold buckle (above) depicts a dancing satyr with a bunch of grapes, while the frame is formed from facing horse heads; 4th century AD.

established in Britain again for another 200 years, and bronze coin would not circulate again until the seventeenth century.

Yet to complicate matters, the idea that the province was in decline is by no means evident everywhere. In fact, the fourth century AD has been termed by some Britain's 'Golden Age', because much of the high-quality material culture dates to this time. There are a number of hoards of late Roman gold and silver which demonstrate that a few people were able to accrue huge amounts of wealth. The Hoxne treasure, for example, found in 1992, is the largest hoard of Roman gold and silver from Britain, and indeed one of the largest in the Roman empire (figs. 117, 119). Comprising almost 16,000 gold and silver coins, gold jewellery and small items of silver tableware – all buried in a wooden box – it evidently belonged to a family of some considerable standing. Indeed, the owners are likely to have had direct connections with the

121 A silver dining service from Mildenhall, Suffolk, buried around the late 4th century AD, and found by a farmer during World War II (1939–45).

'THE GREAT DISH', *a platter decorated at its centre with the head of the sea god Oceanus, surrounded by sea creatures. The outer frieze depicts Bacchus, god of wine, and the hero Hercules, with musicians and dancing girls.*

SMALL DISHES, *a pair. The one on the left depicts Pan and a dancing girl (maenad), who plays a double flute; the other dish (opposite) shows a young satyr dancing with a maenad, who plays a tambourine.*

FLUTED BOWL, *with a six-pointed star at its centre. It was probably filled with water for washing hands at table.*

DEEP BOWLS, *one of four (above and opposite), with flat rims decorated with hunting scenes and characters from Roman mythology.*

LADLES *with round bowls, and handles in the shape of dolphins.*

PLATTER, *with the central roundel and rim decorated with geometric designs and rosettes, inlaid with niello (silver sulphide), to contrast with the silver.*

DANCING GIRL (MAENAD) *holding a staff, with the long train of her dress arching around her head. Her hair is held in a typically Roman, tight bun, and she wears a garland of flowers and leaves.*

PEDESTAL PLATTERS, *a pair, with beaded rims and geometric decoration, elaborate stems and cup-shaped bases.*

A TRITON *(Roman sea deity) blowing a conch shell forms the lid-handle of a covered serving bowl.*

SMALL BOWL, *one of a pair, its rim richly decorated with a vine scroll containing leaves, flowers, grapes, birds and rabbits.*

Imperial Court, for precious metal at this time was controlled by the emperor, and ownership of it usually came as a result of imperial favour.

Hoxne is not alone, for at Mildenhall in Suffolk, a late Roman silver dining service was discovered when struck by a ploughman in the winter of 1942. Evidence for dining on a lavish scale, it has yet to be surpassed in Britain in terms of the quality of its Classical decoration (fig. 121). The Corbridge *lanx* is the sole survivor of another hoard of top-quality silver objects (fig. 118). At Thetford, Norfolk, a large set of silver spoons and gem-encrusted gold jewellery was found in what was probably a cult sanctuary to the Roman god Faunus (fig. 120). As we have seen, a set of silver vessels was also buried at Water Newton, and probably belonged to an early Christian community, demonstrating that wealth could be accumulated by private individuals or for use in communal ownership (fig. 108). At Burgh Castle, a Saxon-shore fort on the east Norfolk coast

122 BELOW *Aerial view of the Saxon-shore fort at Burgh Castle, Norfolk; late 3rd to early 4th century AD (see also fig. 124) (© Adrian Warren/Lastrefuge.co.uk).*

(fig. 122), a set of glass drinking vessels, buried in a pit, is a remarkable survival, given their fragility, and some of the vessels are probably among the 'latest' items to be made in the province (fig. 124). These deposits of precious objects are heavily concentrated in eastern Britain. In the west, instead,

different signs of wealth appear in the form of several extremely affluent villas, some with extensive and accomplished mosaics. One of the most densely packed regions is Gloucestershire, and particularly the Cotswold Hills, which have produced evidence of about fifty villas, some of which are spectacularly ornate, and a number of which are new foundations of the late third and fourth century. Woodchester, for instance, had at least sixty-four rooms and contained the largest British mosaic known, composed of around one and a half million tesserae. All this evidence hints at a dense concentration of affluence, and shows that, by the end of the Roman period in Britain, some parts of the country had been completely transformed.

Yet it seems that all of these villas in the west of Britain had been abandoned by the middle of the fifth century AD at the very latest, and this is also the period by which all of the hoards of gold and silver had

been buried in the east. The hoards indicate that a point was reached when it was probably no longer deemed wise to keep hold of these objects, as being caught with them was potentially dangerous. All these hoards were buried, probably for later recovery, although in some cases there may have been a religious motive – the placing of the material under 'divine' protection or 'gifting' to the gods in the hope of salvation. The increasing vulnerability of the province to 'barbarian' attack was no doubt a factor, but we should also consider the possibility of internal strife, which made the wealthy feel insecure, particularly as the military presence had significantly declined after the time of Constantine III (AD 407–11). There is no archaeological evidence of a 'peasant revolt', and certainly none for full-scale civil war, but localized sporadic uprisings against the ruling elite by an assortment of escaped slaves, bandits and disgruntled soldiers, should not be ruled out.

But what of the period after Britain had been left to govern herself? For many years, it seemed that the century or so following AD 410 was virtually invisible in archaeological terms, but in recent years a number of new discoveries have begun to fill the gap. In 1997, a highly unusual coin hoard was found at Patching in West Sussex at the site of a prehistoric hillfort and Anglo-Saxon cemetery (fig. 123). What makes Patching atypical is the 'lateness' of its contents: in addition to two plain gold finger rings and some items of scrap silver, there were 23 gold *solidi* and 23 silver *siliquae* (coins) of Honorius, his successor Valentinian III

(AD 425–55) and Theodosius II (AD 408–50), with the latest coin in the hoard struck by Libius Severus in AD 465. It was likely buried around AD 470, during the period when our evidence for material culture is very insubstantial.

These visible traces of individual people are given even greater clarity by another recent find. At Ringlemere in Kent, excavations were initiated after the discovery of a Bronze Age gold cup (fig. 8). As is often the case, instead of the expected Bronze Age activity, an Anglo-Saxon graveyard was found comprising fifty-one burials. Other Anglo-Saxon graveyards are well documented, the most famous being the burial mounds at Sutton Hoo, but most of these date to the sixth and seventh centuries AD. Ringlemere is different because of its very early Anglo-Saxon date: all of the material from the graveyard, including beads, buckles, brooches and an intact glass claw beaker (fig. 125), dates between about AD 450 and 620. The graveyard thus provides some of the first clear

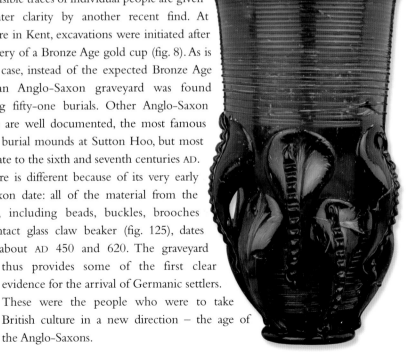

125 RIGHT *Glass claw beaker from an Anglo-Saxon cemetery excavated at Ringlemere, Kent; mid-5th century AD.*

evidence for the arrival of Germanic settlers. These were the people who were to take British culture in a new direction – the age of the Anglo-Saxons.

TIMELINE 55BC–c.AD410

BC

55–4   Julius Caesar makes two unsuccessful attempts to invade Britain. Commios is installed as a tribal leader in the south.

54 BC–AD 43   Britain exports a range of goods to the Continent and receives Continental products, such as wine and metalwork in exchange. A succession of tribal leaders (e.g. Cunobelin and Tincomarus), some friendly to Rome, control different parts of Britain.

AD

*c.*40   Death of Cunobelin.

42   British tribal leader, Verica, seeks refuge in Rome.

43   Claudius invades Britain and defeats British forces as the Roman army make for Colchester. Eleven British kings surrender and Claudius is honoured in Rome.

43–7   Expansion of Roman territories to the west and into the Midlands under the commanders Vespasian and Aulus Plautius.

58–60   Campaigns against Welsh tribes, ending in attack on Druid stronghold on Anglesey.

60–1   Boudican revolt, leading to the destruction of Colchester, London and St. Albans. Major reprisals on the Roman side after the revolt is suppressed.

77–83   Campaigns of Agricola in Wales, north England and the Scottish Lowlands. Advance in the east Highlands culminates in the Battle of Mons Graupius, somewhere in north-east Scotland.

92–120   Most of the Vindolanda Tablets are written.

122   Hadrian visits Britain. Hadrian's Wall is constructed following his visit.

139–42   Establishment of the Antonine Wall after Roman advance into Strathmore and Lowland Scotland under the new emperor Antoninus Pius.

181–5   Incursions by tribes north of Hadrian's Wall, which are repulsed. The emperor Commodus commemorates victory in Britain on his coinage.

192–7   Commodus and his successor, Pertinax, a former British governor, are assassinated. Septimius Severus and Clodius Albinus vie for power, and Albinus is defeated. Severus divides Britain into two provinces.

208–11   Revolt in the northern military zone leads to campaigns of Septimius Severus in Scotland. Severus dies in York (211) and his sons, Geta and Caracalla, withdraw.

235–80   Crisis across the whole Roman Empire, with frequent civil wars.

260–74   Britain forms part of the 'Gallic Empire' under Postumus and his successors.

286–95   Carausius is appointed to defend against piracy in the Channel, but rebels and declares himself emperor, controlling Britain and northern Gaul. He is assassinated by his finance minister, Allectus, who is also declared emperor by his troops.

296   Constantius I retakes Britain.

305–6   Constantius I campaigns in northern Britain. After his death at York, his son, Constantine I, is declared emperor.

315	Constantine I is declared *Britannicus* on his coins, showing he had won a military victory in the province. Around this time Britain is divided into four provinces.
342–3	Visit to Britain by the emperor Constans, probably because of trouble in the north.
350–3	Revolt of Magnentius in Gaul, with British support.
367–78	The 'Barbarian Conspiracy', with Britain under attack from all sides. Count Theodosius restores order in north and south Britain.
383?	Magnus Maximus defeats the Scotti and Picti.
396–8	General Stilicho campaigns in Britain against the Scotti and Picti.
406–7	British usurpers, including Constantine III, deplete troops in Britain in their attempts to become emperor.
408–9	Britain under attack from the Saxons.
*c.*410	Britain is left to defend herself and is no longer administered by Rome.

FURTHER READING

Written sources

S. Ireland *Roman Britain: A Sourcebook* (3rd edition, Routledge, 2008)

The Roman Inscriptions of Britain (RIB):

   Vol. I: R.G. Collingwood and R.P Wright (Oxford University Press, 1965);

   Vol. II: S.S. Frere, R.S.O. Tomlin *et al.* (Alan Sutton, 1990–5);

   Vol. III: R.S.O. Tomlin, R.P. Wright and M.W.C. Hassall (Oxbow Books, 2009)

Vindolanda Tablets: see web resources on p. 158.

Prehistoric background

R. Bradley *The Prehistory of Britain and Ireland* (Cambridge University Press, 2007)

B. Cunliffe *Iron Age Britain* (English Heritage/Batsford, 2004)

Roman Britain

J. Alcock *Life in Roman Britain* (English Heritage/Batsford, 1999)

L. Allason-Jones *Daily Life in Roman Britain* (Greenwood, 2008)

G. de la Bédoyère *Roman Britain: A New History* (Thames and Hudson, 2010)

Britannia: A journal of Romano-British and Kindred Studies. Annually from 1974 (Vol. I)

J. Creighton *Britannia: The Creation of a Province* (Routledge, 2006)

A.S. Esmonde Cleary *The Ending of Roman Britain* (Routledge, 2000)

D. Mattingly *An Imperial Possession: Britain in the Roman Empire, 54 BC–AD 409* (Penguin, 2006)

M. Millett *Roman Britain* (English Heritage/Batsford, revised edition, 2005)

T. Potter and C. Johns *Roman Britain* (British Museum Press, 2002)

P. Salway *The Oxford Illustrated History of Roman Britain* (Oxford University Press, 1993)

M. Todd (ed) *A Companion to Roman Britain* (Blackwell, 2004)

R. J. A. Wilson *A Guide to the Roman Remains in Britain* (4th edition, Constable, 2002)

Post-Roman Britain

S. Glasswell *The Earliest English: Living and Dying in Early Anglo-Saxon England* (Tempus, 2002)

Specific subjects

L. Allason-Jones *Women in Roman Britain* (2nd revised edition, Council for British Archaeology, 2005)

D. Allen *Roman Glass in Britain* (Shire, 1998)

G. de la Bédoyère *Architecture in Roman Britain* (Shire, 2002)

G. de la Bédoyère *Eagles Over Britannia* (Tempus, 2001)

G. de la Bédoyère *Pottery in Roman Britain* (Shire, 2004)

P. Bidwell *Roman Forts in Britain* (Tempus, 2007)

A. Birley *Garrison Life at Vindolanda: A Band of Brothers* (Tempus, 2002)

A. Birley *The People of Roman Britain* (Batsford, 1979)

R. Birley *Vindolanda, a Roman Frontier Fort on Hadrian's Wall* (Amberley, 2009)

A.K. Bowman *Life and Letters on the Roman Frontier: Vindolanda and its People* (British Museum Press, 2003)

D. J. Breeze and B. Dobson *Hadrian's Wall* (4th revised edition, Penguin, 2000)

H. Cool *Eating and Drinking in Roman Britain* (Cambridge University Press, 2006)

H. Davies *Roman Roads in Britain* (Shire, 2008)

M. J. Green *The Gods of Roman Britain* (Shire, 2003)

M. Henig *Religion in Roman Britain* (Batsford, 1984; Taylor & Francis e-Library, 2005)

M. Henig *The Art of Roman Britain* (Batsford, 1995; Taylor & Francis e-Library, 2003)

C. Johns *The Jewellery of Roman Britain: Celtic and Classical Traditions* (University College London Press, 1996)

D. E. Johnston *Roman Villas* (Shire, 2004)

R. Reece *The Coinage of Roman Britain* (Tempus, 2002)

P. R. Sealey *The Boudican Revolt Against Rome* (Shire, 2004)

E. Swift *Roman Dress Accessories* (Shire, 2003)

Web resources

http://vindolanda.csad.ox.ac.uk (Vindolanda Tablets)

www.britishmuseum.org/explore/galleries/europe/room_49_roman_britain.aspx (The Weston Gallery of Roman Britain, the British Museum)

www.finds.org.uk/ (The Portable Antiquities Scheme)

www.hadrians-wall.org/ (the official Visiting Hadrian's Wall website)

www.museumoflondon.org.uk/English/Collections/OnLineResources/Londinium (Living in Roman London)

www.potsherd.uklinux.net/ (Pottery in Roman Britain)